The ROUGH GUIDE to the Best Android™ apps

by Andrew Clare

www.roughguides.com

Credits

**The Rough Guide to
the Best Android Apps**

Text and design: Andrew Clare
Editing: Kate Berens
Proofreading: Anita Sach
Production: Gemma Sharpe

Rough Guides Reference

Director: Andrew Lockett
Editors: Kate Berens,
Tom Cabot, Tracy Hopkins,
Matt Milton, Joe Staines

Publishing information

This first edition published August 2012 by
Rough Guides Ltd, 80 Strand, London, WC2R 0RL
Email: mail@roughguides.com

Distributed by the Pengion Group:
Penguin Group (USA), 375 Hudson Street, NY 10014, USA
Penguin Group (India), 11 Community Centre, Panchsheel Park, New Delhi 110017, India
Penguin Group (Australia), 250 Camberwell Road, Camberwell, Victoria 3124, Australia
Penguin Group (New Zealand), 67 Apollo Drive, Rosedale, Auckland 0632, New Zealand

Rough Guides is represented in Canada by Tourmaline Editions Inc.,
662 King Street West, Suite 304, Toronto, Ontario M5V 1M7

Printed and bound in Singapore by Toppan Security Printing Pte. Ltd.
Typeset in Minion and Myriad
Cover design: Andrew Clare

© Andrew Clare, 2012
192 pages; includes index

A catalogue record for this book is available from the British Library.

ISBN: 978-1-40936-269-2

1 3 5 7 9 8 6 4 2

Contents

Introduction

There are now more than 450,000 apps rubbing shoulders on Google Play™ (formerly known as the Android Market™) – from seasoned stalwarts that have been around for years to the innovative upstarts snapping at their heels. And there are a lot of mediocre efforts to sift through in order to find the good stuff. So we figured it was time to put together a comprehensive list of the best apps currently out there in each and every category.

Whether you're a business type looking to maximize your mobile productivity, a parent looking for a way to keep your toddler entertained in the back of the car, or a recent Android™ convert looking for the best games and social networking apps, you'll find what you're looking for among these pages.

This book assumes a working knowledge of the Android platform. We've included a chapter on using Google Play and alternative services to install apps, but if you find yourself struggling with other concepts within this book, you might find the *Rough Guide to Android Phones & Tablets* a useful addition to your library.

About this book

Text written like **this** denotes a command or label as it appears on screen. Something written like **this** refers to the name of an app or widget that can be downloaded from Google Play™ or other source.

This book was written using a Samsung Galaxy Nexus phone running Android™ 4.0. Most of the apps reviewed will work on devices running Android 2.2 or later, but we cannot guarantee that everything mentioned will work with your specific device.

Most (but not all) of the apps mentioned in this book are either free or offer a free, trial or ad-supported "lite" version; others may appear to be free when installing but require in-app purchases in order to unlock full functionality. We've eschewed listing actual prices as these vary between territories and are often subject to change. Some of the features mentioned in the reviews may exist only in the paid version, so check the full feature lists from Google Play when installing apps if there's a particular function you're after.

Acknowledgements

Thanks to Kate Berens, Peter Buckley, Andrew Lockett and Iris Balija for their help and encouragement.

Managing apps
Google Play and more

In this chapter we'll give you a brief introduction on how to browse and install apps using Google Play™. We'll show you how to use the Play Shop app on your device (this may be called Market on older devices, but it should behave in much the same way), and the Google Play web interface. We'll also throw in a few tips and tricks, as well as discussing a few other sources for finding apps.

Using the Play Shop app

The **Play Shop** app will have been pre-installed on your Android™ device. If you can't see it on your home screen, you'll find it hiding in the app tray. Opening up the Play Shop, you'll see an arrangement of panels advertising various "featured" apps and games, along with some smaller panels in the middle of the screen, linking to Google Play's Apps, Games, Books, Movies and (in the US, at least) Music sections. You may also see links to Staff and Editors' Choices.

Browsing apps

Swipe left and right or tap the tabs to shunt between Featured Apps, Top Paid, Top Free and other charts. At the far left you'll find the Categories page, which lists everything in a slightly more useful manner (games, books, business, entertainment and so on, more or less the same categories as you'll find in this book).

You'd be forgiven for finding the Play Shop a tad labyrinthine. If you can't find what you're after, simply tap on the magnifying glass button to enter a search term, or you can tap the microphone to perform a voice search.

Installing a free app

Select any app from your search and you'll be taken to a screen showing a few lines about what it does, how much of your device's memory it'll use, and some screenshots that you can flick through or tap on for a closer look.

Scrolling down the page, you'll see a handful of the most recent user reviews and ratings.

Tip: It's worth reading through a few of the user ratings as they'll often give you some indication of any problems the app may have on certain devices, or if it's just plain not worth bothering with.

You'll either see an **Install** or a **Download** button at the top of the screen. Tapping it takes you to a list of the services and functions the app will access. Give this list a quick once-over and tap **Accept & download** to install the app. A small animated ⬆ will appear in the notification bar while it's downloading, changing to a ☑ once the app is installed. From there on, your new app can be found in the apps list (**Menu > My apps**) or can be placed on your home screen for easy access.

App windows just keep on going: this is less than half of the information you can wade through when perusing a potential download.

> **Tip:** You can search for apps directly from the Google™ Search bar, without having to load up the Play Shop app.

Installing a paid app

Installing a paid app follows much the same process as for a free app, but with an extra few steps the first time around.

Instead of the **Install** button at the bottom of the app's screen, you'll see a button with its price in your local currency. Tapping this takes you to a Google Checkout™ screen asking you for credit card details. You can enter these here or, preferably, take a minute or two out to set up a Google Checkout account on your computer (see box, opposite).

Once you've entered your details you'll see a message that the transaction is being authorized. Your phone will ring at this stage, and you'll hear a friendly robot at the other end of the line asking you some personal details in order to verify your purchase. Answer the robot's questions nicely.

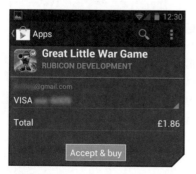

Once your details are registered with Google Checkout™ you'll never need to enter them again, and installing paid apps is pretty much the same speedy process as for free ones.

Google Checkout

If you already have a Google account, setting up Google Checkout™ only takes a minute. Checkout acts as an intermediary, handling your Google Play™ payments for you and passing these charges on to your credit or debit card. It's a free service that can be used with an increasing number of online retailers and means you don't have to keep setting up new accounts or handing your card details out all over the Internet.

That's it! You can now download and start using the app. Meanwhile you'll get a confirmation email sent to your Gmail™ account.

Many paid apps have a free trial version you can check out first, but if there's no such trial available for an app you're interested in, you have a slight buffer against wasting your money by returning the app for a refund.

Act fast for a refund

If you decide that the new app isn't quite your cup of tea, you can return to its page (via the **Menu > My apps** in the Play Shop) within fifteen minutes of making your purchase, where you'll find an **Uninstall and refund** button near the top of the screen. Another message sent to your Gmail account will provide confirmation once you're done.

Will every app work with my device?

Probably not; the slowness of some manufacturers and mobile carriers to update to the latest version of Android™ means that users of older phones and tablets may find themselves left behind as newer apps come out that only support more recent releases of the platform. Some developers also place geographic restrictions on their apps, meaning you won't be able to install them in certain territories (although you can sometimes get around this, see p.20). Finally, some apps are just badly written, while others have known problems with specific devices.

Browsing apps from your computer

Browsing the Play Shop from the small screen of a phone or tablet is about as user-friendly as it could be under the circumstances, but for a less cramped experience, fire up your computer's web browser and direct it to play.google .com. Once there, you'll find the same apps, games and widgets, but presented via a much friendlier interface.

Installing from the web interface

The **Install** button can be found in the top left of the screen, in the square panel where the app's title is. If an app needs paying for it'll have a button showing the price

The Google Play™ webpage (above) lets you browse from the relative comfort of a full-size computer screen. Most of the important information can be accessed from the same screen, and everything else is available from the tabbed centre panel.

You only need to buy apps once

If you factory-reset your phone or tablet, switch to another one or have multiple Android™ devices, you won't have to pay more than once for your apps.

Log in to Google Play™ with the same Google™ login that you use for your other devices, and you'll see all your previously downloaded apps in the **My Android Apps** section. From here you can reinstall any of your apps and those you've already paid for will be available for free.

instead. Upon clicking the button, you'll be taken to a checkout window. Select the device you'd like to install to (if you have more than one) from the drop-down menu. The window also lists which permissions the app requires. Give this a quick look to make sure it's not overstepping the mark (see box on p.18), and then hit the **Install** button. Assuming your device is switched on with a working Internet connection, it will be downloaded, installed and ready to use the next time you connect. If not, it'll download at the next available opportunity.

Other ways to install apps

AppBrain

To use this popular alternative to Google Play™, you'll need to install and run the **AppBrain App Market**

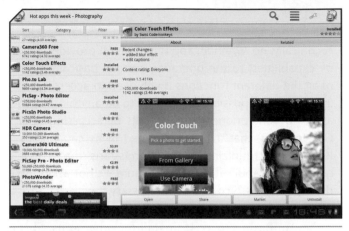

AppBrain was ahead of the curve when it came to providing a web interface for installing and uninstalling apps to Android™ devices. Google™'s own Play web interface has finally caught up, but AppBrain retains many loyal followers and still seems to be the only service that enables you to uninstall via the web.

and **Fast Web Installer** apps (search for "AppBrain" on Google Play). Log in to the **AppBrain App Market** app using your Google™, Facebook or Twitter account settings and give your approval for the Fast Web Installer to do its thing.

Once you've set this up you can browse to appbrain .com on your computer and start installing apps to your Android device. You can also uninstall apps directly from the website via the **My Apps** section (Google Play currently only allows you to uninstall apps from your device). Click **Cancel Install** for apps that you've installed

Can apps contain viruses?

Technically, no. When an app is installed it provides a list of "capabilities" to the operating system, basically a list of all the different functions it will need to access. Once installed, it's impossible for the app to do anything (such as using your phone to make calls or accessing your GPS location) that it hasn't declared in its capabilities. It's worth scrutinizing these permissions that you're granting the application, to make sure it's not asking to do anything you'd consider unnecessary.

via the AppBrain site, or **Uninstall** for other apps. Firing up AppBrain on your device, tap **Manage my apps > Sync with AppBrain** to see a list of pending uninstalls. Tapping **Perform installs** will set any queued installs or uninstalls in action.

Tip: When looking at paid apps, shop around between download sites and the official Google Play store – the app you want may be available more cheaply or even for free.

Amazon

The Amazon Appstore (only available in the US at the time of writing) works in much the same way as Google Play or AppBrain, with the added convenience that you may already have a credit card set up with Amazon. To install Amazon's own **Appstore** app, head to the Appstore website, try to install something and you'll be prompted for your email address. A link to the Appstore app will then be emailed to you. Before you can install it, you'll need to head to **Settings > Security** and make sure the **Unknown sources** box is ticked. One of the best things about Amazon's Appstore is their daily free or discounted app offers – worth keeping an eye on for some great deals.

▶ **Amazon Appstore** goo.gl/LOYR1

Other non-Google app sources

Many of the sites below have their own Play Shop-like apps that allow you to install stuff in pretty much the same way as the official one.

▶ **GetJar Gold** getjar.com/gold

▶ **Handango** handango.com

▶ **Phoload** phoload.com

▶ **Soc.io Mall** mall.soc.io

▶ **SlideMe** slideme.org

Alternatively you can search and download .apk files directly from the web and install them with the help of an app such as **Easy Installer**. Or use a file manager app (see p.148), most of which will let you install apps from SD memory; if you have one, dig deep into its features to see if it has that capability.

Installing restricted apps

If there's an app you'd like to try out but for some reason it's unavailable in your country, you can often circumnavigate this restriction using the following method.

On your Android device, open up a web browser, head to play.google.com and search for the app in question. When you've found it, hit the **Install** button as if installing from a desktop web browser. At this stage your device should ask you which app you'd like to use in order to perform the action; select **Play Shop** and you should be able to continue your installation as normal from there.

This works because the Play Shop app restricts apps simply by hiding them from your searches; perform the first half of the process from a web browser and you're in through the back door. Google may well fix this little loophole at some point in the future, but for now, it works.

Books and comics

Words and pictures

Digital publishing is a mishmash of proprietary and open formats, and hardware (and software) eReaders. If you already own a Kindle, Nook, Kobo, Sony Reader or one of the other brands of eBook reader, your allegiances are probably already set. Each have apps that you can grab from Google Play™ to access your existing library. While you're at it, download a good all-rounder like Mantano or Moon+Reader that will serve you for everything else.

 ### Kobo

Syncs with your Kobo account and any other eBooks stored on your device. You can highlight passages and add notes, but display options are quite rudimentary. Kobo also collects your reading statistics and issues award badges for milestones such as finishing a book, reading through the night, and other dubious achievements.

Google Books

Google™'s own eBook reader plays nicely (and exclusively) with the Google Play™ Books store and has a useful range of display settings, including the option to read a book from scans of its original pages. It doesn't, however, offer anything in the way of highlighting or note-taking.

Nook

Barnes and Noble's Nook app includes magazine and newspaper subscriptions, and allows in-app book lending to your friends (with limitations, but it's a step in the right direction compared to other services).

Amazon Kindle

Useful if you already purchase books, newspapers and magazines from the Kindle store, but won't import anything else. The Kindle app is otherwise well rounded with highlights, notes, dictionary look-up, and a rudimentary PDF viewer.

Mantano

Lightning fast and with a ton of features, Mantano is a PDF and ePub reader that looks great on tablets. Features include customizable themes you can apply to books; a well laid-out, searchable library, allowing you to add tags and organize books into categories; text highlighting; shareable quotes and annotations; text-to-speech; dictionary search; an excellent range of view modes for PDF, and more.

Moon+ Reader

Will handle just about any format you can throw at it. This superb reader supports display themes, highlights and annotations, bookmarks, auto-scroll, Dropbox sync and tons of display and navigation customizations. For a similar feature set, **Cool Reader** is also worth a look.

WattPad

Also known as "YouTube™ for eBooks", Wattpad lets you browse, read, rate and comment on over a million community-submitted stories, poems and books. Feeling brave? Create a free account and start submitting your own work.

Overdrive Media Console

Borrow and read eBooks and audiobooks from your public, school or college library. Borrowed titles expire automatically so there are never any late fees, and a countdown clock shows you how many days you have left for any given book.

Audible

If audiobooks are more your kind of thing, look no further. Audible's digital store currently hosts over one hundred thousand titles in all genres. You can start listening while still downloading, add bookmarks and even vary the narration speed. For a standalone player, try **Smart AudioBook Player**.

PDF readers

ezPDF Reader

If you're after something a bit more capable than your average free PDF viewer, ezPDF is worth paying for. It displays accurately, has sensible small-screen enhancements, and lets you add annotations and work with forms. It also features a night mode (inverting text onto a black background and making images grayscale) which is both easy on the eye, and on your device's battery. A free cloud plugin syncs your files with Google Docs™. At a slightly higher price point, **RepliGo Reader** has a similarly full feature set.

Adobe Reader

Adobe's own free reader has enough functionality to keep the average user happy. It's fast, accurate, displays annotations, sticky notes and drawing markups, and includes a search feature, bookmarks and continuous scroll display. It also lets you read encrypted, password-protected and DRM rights-managed PDFs.

Comics

Comics by Comixology

Comixology's combined viewer, library and store app gives you access to its huge digital library from publishers including Marvel and DC (both of which have their own Comixology-powered apps on Google Play™), Image, IDW, Archie and more. The viewer includes useful small-screen optimizations and Guided View, which automatically moves between frames to avoid unnecessary zooming and swiping around the page.

Droid Comic Viewer

Compact but versatile free comic and manga reader. It supports most formats, has an excellent no-fuss user interface and works like a dream.

Comica

Stunning all-round comic and image viewer supporting a sensible range of formats. In contrast to the Droid Comic Viewer, it takes more of a bells-and-whistles approach, with a beautiful user interface, thumbnail library display, snapshots, and more.

Business
Off to work we go

Whatever your line of work, you'll find apps that can make your job a lot easier, from office suites and invoicing for people on the move, to specialist tools for designers, landlords, hairdressers (no, not virtual scissors), plumbers and just about any other vocation.

Tracking & Logging

Gleeo Time tracker
Simple time recording tool that lets you break down a project into as many component activities as you like and separately time-track each. You can easily track multiple projects and access statistics over an animated timeline.

Barcode & Inventory Pro

Ideal for keeping track of your inventory of books, DVDs, or any other barcode-labelled items. You can manage your inventory with tags, categories, by location, price and more. Attach photos or icons to items, import product details from Amazon and Google™ and export to a range of formats including Google Docs™ and CSV. It's also worth looking at **Inventory Tracker** to compare which app suits your needs, or for a free alternative, try **Inventory**.

Parcels

Allows you to track parcels from all the major shipping services in the US and UK. Track multiple packages, labelled and colour-coded for easy reference, and receive detailed status updates. It can even display progress on a Google Map™. Want more? Check out **TrackChecker**.

Invoicing

Invoice2Go

Make fast, professional-looking invoices, credit memos and purchase orders from customizable templates and email them as PDFs (including optional PayPal buttons for instant payment). Invoice2Go calculates totals and taxes based on your location and currency and helps you keep track of what you're owed. The free version restricts you to storing three invoices at a time, any more than that and you'll need to delete them or buy the full app. As an alternative, try **Zoho Invoice**, which is free for up to five invoices per month, with monthly fees kicking in above that.

Mobile Biz Pro

As well as providing a complete mobile PDF invoicing solution, this lets you track customer balances, send statements and receipts, and take handwritten signatures directly into your device for approval of estimates or purchase orders. It can also generate reports based on, for example, customer or item profitability. Add on barcode scanning, inventory management, payment tracking and PayPal buttons, and you're covered for running your business in the field.

Meetings

 ### Adobe Connect Mobile

Lets you host and attend online meetings from your tablet or smartphone, with two-way video conferencing, live text chat, content and screen sharing and more. The host of the meeting will need an Adobe Connect account, while other attendees can simply join as guests.

 ### CallTrack

Keeps a log of your phone activity and sends a record of calls, dates and durations to your Google Calendar™. Useful if you need a permanent record of who you spoke to and when.

Meeting REC

Helps you keep a record of a meeting's minutes in case you don't happen to have a dedicated clerk handy. Its in-built multiple voice recorder and timeline lets you manually tag the voices of up to eight participants as the meeting progresses, so that you can review later to see exactly who said what, and when.

Contacts & Calendar

Jorte
Pleasant-looking and easy to use personal organizer-style calendar replacement. Has most of the functionality of the stock app with added tasks, schedules, and more. It may take a little tweaking to get it syncing with your Google Calendar™, but it's well worth the effort.

Business Calendar
Zoomable calendar app that syncs with your Google Calendar™. If you like the look of the new Calendar in Android 4.0 but can't get it on your device, this app has a very similar look and feel. Supports recurring items, drag and drop, multiple views, contact linking to events, and more.

Touchdown HD
Outlook-like app for Microsoft Exchange accounts, bringing email, contacts, calendars and tasks, notes and SMS together into a single tabbed interface. It's fully customizable with an impressive array of widgets. An excellent all-in-one solution for corporate users. Exchange users looking for a good all-round sync solution should try **RoadSync**.

Quick Event
Quick Event lets you quickly add events by voice entry. It supports recurring events, date-spanning

and other complex details. You can say something like "On location from 2pm tomorrow until 5am Friday, in London," and the event will be created with times, dates and location all present and correct.

Office suites

Documents To Go

View, edit and create Microsoft Word (.doc and .docx), Excel (.xls and .xlsx), PowerPoint (.ppt) and Adobe PDF files (its PDF viewer is one of the best available). Impressively sophisticated for its size, it offers features like word count, find on page, formatting tools, word wrap, multiple zoom levels and track changes, and support for password-protected files. There's also a Live Folder facility that puts a recently used files folder on your home screen. It also syncs and edits Google Docs™ files with ease. There are a handful of other excellent office suites available from Google Play™, all offering similar tools and features with varying strengths and weaknesses. Take a look at trial versions of **Quickoffice Pro** and **Kingsoft Office** as well before making a purchase.

Sheet To Go - ACME Expense Report.xlsx

A1 | Expense Report

Expense Report

Date	Travel	Meals&En
May 19-20	$988.40	$391.54
09-May-10	$460.40	$0.00
18-May-10	$60.00	$0.00
18-May-10	$0.00	$16.05
18-May-10	$0.00	$12.26
18-May-10	$0.00	$13.23
18-May-10	$0.00	$0.00
18-May-10	$50.00	$0.00
19-May-10	$0.00	$0.00
19-May-10	$0.00	$350.00
20-May-10	$60.00	$0.00
20-May-10	$358.00	$0.00

Expe...ort

Vodafone & MS Office 365
Microsoft Office 365 from Vodafone - Find Out More Today!

Google Docs

Google™'s own tablet-optimized Docs app hooks you up instantly with your Google Docs™ online for viewing and editing spreadsheets, presentations, word and text files, images and more. For a free suite it's excellent for lightweight word processing needs. Anything more complicated (editing spreadsheets, for example) and you'll probably want to look to one of the paid apps.

Print & Scan

Cloud Print

Free app which lets you print wirelessly to any Google Cloudprint™-ready printer, or to any other printer connected to a computer running Google Chrome™. Cloud Print can be a little clunky to set up but works well once you've got it running. Modern printers by Epson, HP, and other manufacturers may have their own Wi-Fi or Bluetooth printing apps, so check Google Play™ for your model to see if it already has a brand-specific solution, or for a slightly smoother paid-for app, try **PrinterShare**.

Scanthing

Use your phone or tablet's camera to quickly capture and OCR-trace text, useful for saving newspaper or magazine articles to editable text from a hard copy. You can also do this with **Google Goggles™** (see p.44) and **Evernote** (p.119).

Cam Scanner

Quickly scans, auto-enhances, crops, tags, converts to PDF, and uploads to Google Docs™, Dropbox or Box.com without jumping between apps. It also supports multiple pages and sizes within the same document. Currently there doesn't seem to be a really good all-in-one solution for OCR-tracing and PDF generation within the same app, but if you need both, try **Document Scanner** as your first port of call.

Other business apps

 ## Project Schedule

Simple, functional project management app that lets you create and edit Gantt charts with task scheduling and support for MS-Project files. You can assign tasks to groups, calculate costs, get notifications about a project's progress and export your charts to CSV or XML formats, or to an image file. For other project management solutions, check out **GanttDroid Pro** and **Project Viewer**.

SignMyPad
Simple, useful signature tool that lets you sign, save and send PDF files without the headache of scanning, printing or faxing, getting one step closer to a paperless office while you're at it.

Web to PDF
This excellent free plugin for the Dolphin web browser (see p.66) is quick, straightforward, and works better than most dedicated converters (including Adobe's) for saving webpages into the PDF format.

Splashtop Remote Desktop
One of many remote desktop apps available (other good choices are **LogMeIn+ Ignition** and **PocketCloud Remote Desktop**), Splashtop works just as happily with Mac or PC, is (relatively) easy to set up, and as well as giving you full remote control of your computer, it can also stream high-quality audio and video to your Android™ device.

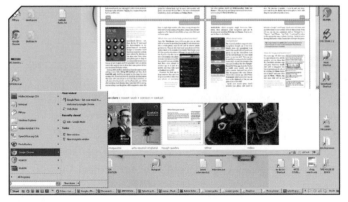

Communication
Email, calls and more

With the dizzying number of ways people can stay in touch these days, it's nice to have access to all of these methods in one place – your smartphone. It's no doubt already set up for SMS, email and phone calls. Add video calling, VoIP and IRC chat and you've got yourself an all-in-one communications centre.

Telephony

Google Voice

(US users only) Google Voice™ is a multi-faceted VoIP telephone service. It gives you a single phone number which you can use forever, irrespective of where you live or which phone services you use. You can also use it to replace your existing voicemail service for the ability to listen to your voicemail online, and receive visual voicemail text or email transcripts of your messages. It also acts as a switchboard for all your phones, letting you route calls to any of your other numbers (landline, mobile, office, etc), or ring multiple numbers at the same time. The service also offers free text messaging and cheap international calls.

GrooVe IP
Lets you use your Google Voice phone number to make free VoIP calls over Wi-Fi and 3G within the US and Canada. It may take some tweaking to get the best sound quality and, as you'd expect, results over 3G can be a little patchy. If you're having sound quality issues, try **gVoice** instead. Alternatively, for another way to get free calls from Google Voice, try the **Google Voice Callback** app.

Mr. Number
Take complete control over incoming calls and texts. Mr. Number lets you block calls and texts from specific numbers or area codes, with a crowd-sourced "suspected spam'" blocklist for automatically blocking telemarketing or other cold calls, or you can simply block anyone not in your contacts list. It also optionally doubles as a one-stop dialler and messaging replacement. For more call blocking options, try **Call Control**.

Viber – free calls & texts
Free calls and texts over Wi-Fi to other Viber users. Feels more like making a regular phone call than Skype does, and the app itself seems a little less resource hungry. **Rebtel** is another app offering free and cheap calls.

Vibe
Vibe lets you set custom vibrate patterns for different contacts, enabling you to feel who's calling you when your phone is set to vibrate. Ideal for meetings, classes, or any other situation where you might not want to pull out your phone to look at it.

Voxer Walkie-Talkie PTT

Turns your phone or tablet into a push-to-talk style walkie-talkie using your Wi-Fi or data connection. Supports both one-to-one and group chat, and also lets you send photos, text and location info. Among other similar apps we tested, **HeyTell** and **TiKL – Touch To Talk** are worth a look too.

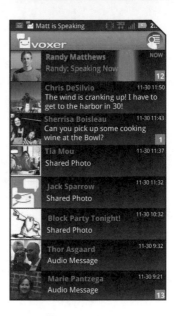

Video calls

Skype

Whichever VoIP service you choose to go with will depend largely on which service most of your contacts are using. And, like it or not, Skype is pretty much ubiquitous. The Skype app for Android™ lets you make free voice and video calls to other Skype users, as well as offering cheap international phone calls.

Tango

Another highly regarded free service. Like Skype, Tango is available on all major platforms, both desktop and mobile. As well as making video and voice calls you can also leave video messages if your recipient doesn't pick up.

Fring

Offers free worldwide video chat, voice calls and live text chat. Where Fring has the edge over other services is that it provides group video chat for up to four users. It's also available on iPhone and iPad, so there's no obstacle to staying in touch with your iFriends.

Google+ Messenger

Google+™ for mobile (see p.136) includes a Messenger facility which lets you join or start a Hangout – basically a live video chat with up to nine friends at the same time. To start a Hangout, initiate a conversation from Messenger and tap the camera icon at the top of the screen. Now all you need is nine friends who actually use Google+.

Messaging

DeskSMS

Lets you send and receive text messages from your computer's web browser, email or IM client, for the convenience of using a full-size keyboard and to save you switching devices. Desktop plugins are available for Firefox and Chrome. Chrome users can also try **MightyText** for an equivalent service.

HeyWire

More a complete messaging hub than an SMS replacement, HeyWire lets you send text messages for free to 45 countries worldwide. It also has Facebook and Twitter chat, handy if you want all of those things in the same place.

Makeloop

With Makeloop you can send out multiple choice polls or simple yes/no questions to a group of contacts via SMS. The app sorts and collates the responses for you, and it can even send an auto-reply and create new contact groups from people who have responded in a certain way. An incredibly useful tool to take the organizational headache out of parties, trips or any other group activity.

Handcent SMS

Powerful, customizable SMS/MMS replacement brimming over with features including: password security; a contact locator (find your friends using GPS); group sending; per-contact notification, ringtone and vibrate settings; themes, skins, emoji and font packs; message scheduling; backup to a Handcent Online account; integrated blacklist for blocking spam; and heaps more. Similar feature sets are also available from **GO SMS Pro** and **chompSMS**, or for a simpler messaging replacement, try **Pansi SMS**.

Kakao

Another stable service which lets users exchange unlimited international text messages for free over Wi-Fi or 3G. You can also send voice, video and photo messages. For an alternative, try **What'sApp**, which offers a very similar service.

Email

K-9 Mail

An open-source replacement for Android™'s stock email app, K-9 Mail supports IMAP, POP3 and MS Exchange (also offered by **Touchdown HD**, p.30). Features include multi-folder sync, flagging, filing, signatures, bcc, PGP encryption and the ability to store mail on your SD card. It will also sync with your Gmail™ account, but doesn't handle labels particularly well. If you're looking to replace your stock email app and don't use Gmail, try this first.

Chat

imo

Consolidate all your online chat identities into one app. Imo lets you chat simultaneously across Facebook Chat, Google Talk™, Skype, MSN, ICQ, AIM, Yahoo!, Jabber, MySpace and more. It supports group chat, multimedia attachments, and can even be used as a walkie-talkie. In our tests we found imo to have a very slight edge over comparable apps **eBuddy Messenger** and **Trillian**, but it's worth checking these out for yourself to see which service you prefer.

Education
Too school for cool

Whatever you're learning – a language, science, practical subject or anything else – you'll find a range of apps that support your studies. Technical calculators, tutorials and organizational study tools sit alongside learning games that help you to internalize your subject without even noticing.

Research

Wikipedia

If you're a terminal looker-upper, look no further. Wikipedia's official app is an invaluable, fast, no-nonsense window on the site's millions of pages of content. A simple search bar at the top of the screen is all you need for the most part. There's also the option to save pages and display nearby places of interest on a map, complete with links to their related entries. For slightly more features, including the ability to add newspapers and other wiki sites, try **Wiki Encyclopedia Pro**.

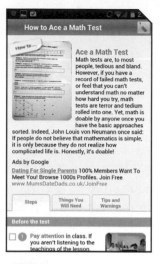

wikiHow

Provides a simple, usable interface for wikiHow's vast library of how-to guides for everything from calming an angry cat to coding a computer virus. Each entry comes with tabs for simple step-by-step instructions, things you'll need, and tips and warnings. Now nothing can stop you (except maybe bullets).

Easy PC Troubleshooter Pro

Computer problems? This handy little app will walk you through troubleshooting the most common problems. It's geared more towards Windows 7 than anything else, but a lot of the advice here can be applied to earlier versions of the OS. More help can be found from JP2014's **Computer Troubleshooter**.

Wolfram Alpha

Get instant expert knowledge and computations from Wolfram Alpha's vast collection of algorithms and data. Areas covered include maths, statistics, physics, chemistry, engineering, acoustics, astronomy, geology, geography, biology, computing, history, culture, media, finance, sports and more. Pretty much everything, in fact. That's right. Everything.

Revision

Flashcards Buddy Pro

Flashcards are an excellent way to help you memorize stuff, but can be impractical to carry around. This app lets you create your own flashcards and organize them to test yourself in a variety of ways. You can save your card sets to your device's SD card, Google Docs™ or email, and import new study sets from Quizlet.com.

Exploration

Anatronica

A detailed, interactive 3D map of human skeletal and muscular anatomy (with more systems being added later). Lets you zoom around, rotate, search, switch layers and views, and see in-depth information for each part. You can also test your knowledge with a built-in quiz section

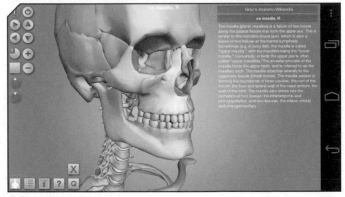

where you identify different bones and muscles from the 3D model. For more bodily explorations, try **Visual Anatomy**.

LHsee

Peruse the latest (admittedly impenetrable) developments from the Large Hadron Collider at CERN, Geneva. The app provides live results in 2D and 3D, along with streaming videos explaining the hunt for the Higgs Boson. It's a nice idea but ultimately feels like watching an episode of Horizon encoded for viewing over Ceefax.

Google Goggles

Lets you perform visual searches by pointing your device's camera at any book, famous building, record, painting or other artefact to get instant identification, along with related search results. It'll OCR-trace a page of text and let you save it, look up addresses, and even translate foreign text and signs into your chosen language. An invaluable tool with a range of applications.

Google Translate

Type or speak your phrase in any language (or simply hand-write on the screen) and have it translated into any other language. For snappier, real-time translation between two tongues, switch to Conversation mode. Google Translate™ also integrates with your sharing options, allowing you to send text from other apps without copy and pasting, and an SMS button can select passages directly from your text messages. A send button will also copy your translation back out to a variety of sources. The closest thing to a universal translator currently available.

Google Earth

Earth is like a supercharged Google Maps™. You can zoom in and out, browse different layers of geographical information, search for sites, businesses and cities, pinpoint your GPS location, and so on. Google Earth™, however, takes all this a step further, with Wikipedia layers, stunning 3D renditions, and a "look around" mode, which lets you rotate around the horizon from your chosen viewpoint.

FactBook

An informative reference app that provides a neat interface for browsing collated information from the CIA World Fact Book and United Nations data and statistics. You can browse or search by region, country or ranking, compare one country to another, and view detailed info and stats on any country in the world, from the population of Papua New Guinea to the military spending of Mexico. Turn your phone on its side while reading about a country and your screen switches to a slideshow of images fetched from Flickr. Want to test your newly acquired knowledge? Try **GeoQuiz**.

Google Sky Map

Turns your phone into a window on the night sky. Simply point in the direction of a star or constellation and the app uses your GPS location and compass to identify it, panning across the cosmos as you move around. You can toggle layers to view stars, planets, grid lines, the horizon and "Messier objects". If you're looking for a particular celestial body, type its name and a pointer will guide you around till you find it. Can't find your home planet? Use the search function to point you in the right direction. For more astronomical intrigue, check out **Celeste** and **Deluxe Moon**.

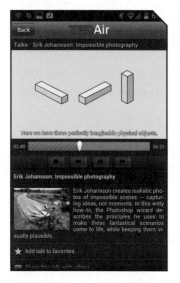

TED Air

There are a few apps out there for accessing TED's fascinating and inspiring lecture content, but TED Air is the best of the lot. Its snappy search engine and ability to find talks by tag or category make finding interesting content a doddle. It also provides subtitles in over eighty languages, and allows you to bookmark, and even download content, for viewing later.

School

School Timetable Deluxe

Keep your school life organized with a nicely designed, customizable lesson planner, viewable by day, week or next subjects. You can also keep track of homework priorities and due dates, and calculate exam grade averages. For more school scheduling, check out **Class Buddy**.

Play

Alchemy

An addictive and (kind of) educational(ish) game that starts you off with the four basic elements of fire, water, earth and air. You drag these around to combine them with each other to make new elements, and then drag those around to combine into other elements. Eventually you'll begin to make more and more complex forms – algae, electricity, vampires – where will it end? Dragging any of these elements into the question mark icon reveals an encyclopedia entry for that item, replete with Wikipedia links to additional information. Educational after all, then.

Finance

Money money money

Not everyone would be entirely comfortable with having easy access to their finances on something as portable as a smartphone, and the idea of keeping log-ins to your accounts on a device that's easily misplaced or stolen does seem somewhat questionable. If you do decide to grant an app access to any sensitive data, be sure you at least have a good lock screen code in place, and a good security app such as avast! (see p.126).

PayPal

The Android™ PayPal app provides some simple tools for securely sending and receiving payments from your PayPal account. Aside from general account management, the app offers a few other features, such as a bill-splitting calculator and the ability to set up payments over NFC by bumping two (NFC-enabled) devices together. US users can find local businesses that accept PayPal payments, and cash a cheque into their PayPal account simply by taking a photo of it.

RpnCalc Financial

Fully functional programmable financial calculator based on the HP 12C (but much, much faster).

Pageonce

Pageonce is a secure web service that lets you consolidate all your financial information – bank accounts, credit cards, bills and investments; track and pay all your bills – with due-date alerts and email reminders – monitor your transactions and view detailed statements; track frequent flyer miles and rewards, and your phone minutes, text and data usage. You can also view detailed reports and charts analysing where your money's going. If you have accounts strewn across the Internet, you can wave goodbye to constantly logging in and out of them all and manage everything from one place. For a worthy alternative, check out the **Mint.com Personal Finance** app.

MoneyWise

MoneyWise is a powerful budget manager (for any currency) that doesn't require an affiliated desktop app or web service to operate properly, allowing you to keep an eye on your cashflow entirely within your Android™ device. It lets you assign budgets for different categories and provides graphs and charts so that you can map your incomings and outgoings with accuracy and ease. What it lacks in visual appeal, it makes up for in functionality and useability.

Bloomberg for Smartphone

Up-to-the-minute market news, data, charts and graphs from one of the most trusted sources. For more, try **Google Finance™** or **Stock Quote**.

Food and drink
Off the eaten track

You've got to eat, right? And you've got to play with your phone, right? Why not combine the two (just not while sitting at the dinner table, thank you very much). Read on for a quick taster of what's available.

Eating out

Urbanspoon

Get local eating recommendations by shaking your phone. Don't like the look of that one? Shake again! If violently shaking an expensive piece of technology for no particularly good reason worries you slightly (and why wouldn't it), you can resort to a good old-fashioned search. As well as being able to filter results by area, food type, rating and so on, you can also select establishments by features such as BYOB, deiivery, free Wi-Fi, kid friendly, vegan friendly and so on.

OpenTable

Check availability and easily make confirmed reservations at an expanding number of restaurants in the UK, US, Canada and Mexico. Members can also earn reward points redeemable at any OpenTable restaurant. Restaurants are searchable by locality or name, and results can be filtered by price, cuisine type or distance. Peruse menus and user reviews to help narrow down your search and book your table, time and party size with just a few taps.

Foodspotting

Looking for somewhere to eat nearby? Foodspotting displays users' photos of dishes from local restaurants, along with ratings and comments. If you like what you see you can tap on the image for a map reference. Create a profile and you can upload your own meals, follow other users and find special offers. For more menu meditations, try **Nosh**.

Kitchen tools

Egg Timer Pro

How do you like your eggs? Simply enter the size of your egg, start temperature and preferred yolk consistency and let the app figure out how long you need to boil it for. It'll even figure out your altitude based on your GPS

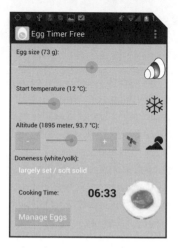

location and factor in the relevant boiling point of water. It's a shame there's currently no facility to share your egg cooking durations with Facebook friends, but that's surely coming in the next update.

Kitchen Math

Excellent cooking utility with unit conversion between US and UK measurements, and volume to weight conversions for more than 380 different ingredients. It'll also convert between Fahrenheit, Celsius and Gas Mark numbers, and suggest perfect serving temperatures for a range of dishes.

Kitchen Timer

No-nonsense multiple kitchen timer you can use to time up to three separate items at once. For a prettier, paid app, try Qweqweq's **Kitchen Timer Pro**.

Recipes

Epicurious

Sensibly curated recipes from the popular food website. The app unfortunately stops short of allowing you to log into your account in order to rate, comment or access saved recipes, but does let you set up a separate favourites list on your Android™ device. One handy feature it does provide is to add recipe ingredients to a shopping list, allowing you to check off those you already have and head out shopping for the rest.

BigOven

Search over 170,000 recipes by keyword or ingredient. You can even list a few leftovers from your fridge and get ideas for how to use them. The app integrates well with a free (but not mandatory) BigOven.com account, letting you rate, review, upload photos and save your own recipes. The interface is clean and friendly, and it's easy to find what you're looking for. If, however, 170,000 recipes isn't quite enough variety for you, try **Recipe Search** or **Dinner Spinner**.

Sweet'N'Spicy

Fancy some of the hot stuff? This app hosts over four thousand searchable Indian recipes, categorized by region, diet (meat, vegetarian or vegan), speed or calorie count. You can list ingredients you have in your kitchen and get instant recipe suggestions, view ratings, watch recipe videos, get useful tips and ask questions of the community.

Ratio

Handy ingredient calculator for when you just want to improvise a meal and need to know the basics of how many parts of this or that to add. Select your food, tell the app how much of each ingredient you have handy, and it'll tell you the rest.

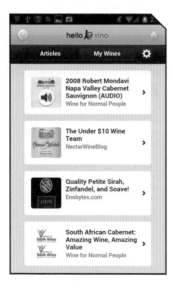

Beer & Wine

Hello Vino

Find a good bottle of wine without peering bewilderedly at the labels on the back. As well as feeding you recommendations and reviews from an easily navigable tree of categories, by occasion, or pairing with a meal, Hello Vino also lets you rate wines, save them for later or order online. Still thirsty? Try **Swirl Pro.**

CAMRA Good Beer Guide 2012

Looking for a decent pint? This app contains over 4500 up-to-date CAMRA-approved UK pubs and breweries (searchable by location and displayed on a trusty Google Map™), with details of beers on offer, food, opening hours and facilities. It also includes reviews and tasting notes for any regular beers served at a particular establishment. To find more beer, try **Cask Finder** or **Untappd**.

Mixology

Mixology has nearly eight thousand drink recipes, well organized and fully searchable. Learn bartending tips and tricks, find local stores and more. You can also type in your available ingredients and see a list of all the cocktails you can currently make.

Barista Me

Let your cup runneth over – with coffee! Barista Me shows common recipes for popular espresso drinks in a beautifully presented graphic interface. Or, if you'd prefer to find a good professional to procure your daily caffeine hit from, try **Bean Hunter**.

Health and fitness

Staying in shape

Whether you're looking for a good night's sleep, motivation to keep fit or some quick medical advice, you'll probably find an app or ten to help you out. Here are a few of the best we could find.

Sleep

Gentle Alarm

An alarm clock that aims to wake you up during light sleep by playing a quiet alarm that kicks in about half an hour before you actually need to wake up. If you're in a shallow part of your sleep cycle you'll hear it and awaken feeling more refreshed than if you'd slept for the full duration.

Sleep Talk Recorder

Worried you might be giving away state secrets while you dream? This app will record any noises you make throughout the night.

Sleep bot Tracker Log

Tracks your sleep patterns and plots them on a graph for analysis. Simply punch in when you're going to sleep and punch out when you wake up. The app figures out your sleep debt and advises you on optimum times to hit the sack. It also provides tips on getting a better night's sleep. Want to silence your phone while you snooze? Try **Sweet Dreams**.

Lightning Bug – Sleep Clock

Ambience and white noise generator to help lull you into slumber, Lightning Bug has over two hundred different sounds, from ocean waves to pulsating synth tones – whatever works… It also has a built-in alarm clock. For more soporific sounds, there's an additional range of plugin packs, or you could try **White Noise** or **Relax and Sleep**.

Sleep as Android

Another sleep timer. This one attempts to measure your sleep patterns using your phone's motion sensor, and like Gentle Alarm, wake you gently at the optimum moment. It also includes a snoring/sleep-talking recorder.

Medical

iTriage

Symptom checker, doctor finder and medical reference tool. First indicate the site of your problem on a picture of a person, and then hone in on your ailment. There's also detailed information about diseases, medications and procedures, along with a user section for saving data, keeping appointments and insurance information. The app's doctor and facility-finding service is mostly US-oriented, but the medical advice and diagnosis information is useful to all. It's also worth looking at **WebMD** and, for UK users, the **NHS Direct** app.

First aid by British Red Cross

This official British Red Cross first aid guide shows you what to do in an emergency, with videos, animations, quizzes and easy-to-follow step-by-step advice. Sensibly organized into learning, testing and preparation sections for more leisurely browsing, along with an emergency section for instant advice in common emergency situations.

ICE: In Case of Emergency

Add information to your phone (people to call, insurance details, doctor's contact details, allergies, medical conditions, any medications you're on and so on) for people to find in the event of an emergency. There are a few apps on Google Play™ that will do this, but Appventive's contribution places a direct link on your lock screen, and emergency contacts can be called directly from the app. It also lets you switch languages while travelling, meaning your information is easily available and understood wherever you roam. There are plenty of free alternatives, such as Sera-Apps' **ICE**, which you can place on your lock screen with the help of the **WidgetLocker** app (see p.102).

Med Helper Pro

Comprehensive medication and appointment reminder to make sure you're taking your prescriptions on time. An alternative is **Pills On The Go**.

Pregnancy & babies

My Pregnancy Today

Enter your due date to get expert day-by-day guidance based on how far along your pregnancy is. Learn what's going on right now, what to expect in the coming days or weeks, and how to cope. Includes foetal development images, a pregnancy checklist with an appointment schedule and reminders, videos, due date calculator, a nutrition guide, and a thriving online community, so you can connect with other women due at the same time.

The app comes with the approval of the international BabyCenter Medical Advisory Board.

Baby ESP

Baby tracker that lets you log your baby's eating, sleeping, diaper changes, medicines and more. After a while you'll be able to see results on a schedule graph, allowing you to anticipate the littl'un's next move and plan accordingly. Also includes a medicine reminder, a daily journal for notes and pictures, detailed statistics, and charts for comparing your baby's progress. As well as helping you get in sync with your baby's needs, it's a useful tool to hand to babysitters so that they have an idea what'll be needed and when. As an alternative, you could try the equally well-made **Baby Connect (tracker)**.

Exercise

CardioTrainer

Free exercise partner for anyone walking, running, biking or doing a wide range of other athletic activities. It lets you work out an exercise schedule, race against yourself to improve times, gives you an estimate of how many calories you've burned, and monitors your activities with GPS tracking and a pedometer. It also has an integrated music player, syncs with a Bluetooth heart rate monitor (manufactured by Polar: goo.gl/XpR8D) and supports a range of (paid) plugins. Core functions are free, while others are trial-only, requiring an upgrade if you wish to continue using them.

 ### Endomondo Sports Tracker

Another excellent sports tracker. In addition to the core features offered by CardioTrainer, Endomondo lets you compete with others for the best times over set routes. Upgrade to the PRO version of the app for graphs, competing against yourself, and the ability to set time and calorie goals with live audio feedback during your workout. For alternatives, try the similarly featured **Runstar** or **Runkeeper**.

 ### Accupedo – Pedometer Widget

As accurate a pedometer app as you're likely to find, this one monitors you daily and logs the number of steps, distances covered, calories burnt and walking time.

Pocket Yoga

Guides you through a yoga session from the convenience of a portable device; you can just plonk it down on the floor in front of you and get, uh, yoga-ing. Sessions are selectable by difficulty level, yoga practice and duration. Spoken instructions accompany pose illustrations and soothing new agey music (you can swap in some death metal from your own music library if you like). Also includes a comprehensive dictionary of poses and (yep, you guessed it), the ability to track your progress on a log. For more, try **A Pose For That**, or any of the excellent **Daily Yoga** modules.

Mind

AmbiScience brainwave apps

Beautifully made brainwave entrainment program, sold in a range of compilations for different uses. AmbiScience apps use binaural beats (basically an incrementally different frequency in each ear) to tune your brain for certain desired states – sleep, meditation, learning, creativity, alertness and more. The effective sounds themselves are hidden within ambient soundtracks and nature noises. Packages are reasonably priced, or you can download a free trial of their Pure Sleep app. For a free alternative, try **Binaural Beats Therapy Beta**.

Memory Trainer

Keep the cogs turning with this gentle mental workout. The app runs you through a series of simple tests, gradually increasing difficulty to task your working memory, "chunking" (ability to break up information into more manageable chunks), spatial memory, focus and concentration skills. For yet more brain training, try **Math Workout** or **Brain Genius Deluxe**.

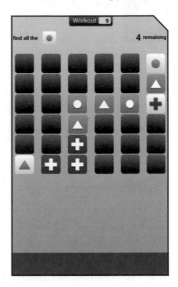

N-Back Maestro

Playing Dual N-Back games can apparently improve fluid intelligence (problem-solving, learning and pattern recognition). The premise of the game is simple: a sequence of objects appear on a three-by-three grid, accompanied by a sound, colour or other variation. All you have to do is compare the current position and variation to the instance two steps back. You then tap a button indicating whether the position or variation (or neither, or both) matches.

For a good free alternative, try **Brain N-Back**. For more brain draining fun try **Brain Age Test Free**.

Insight Timer Meditation Timer
Crystal clear Tibetan singing bowl sounds to accompany your timed meditation session. The app also includes a meditation journal and a feature called Insight Connect, which lets you see how many people around the world are meditating at the same time as you (the ones using this app, at least; you'll have to meditate pretty darn deeply to connect with the rest).

Stop Panic & Anxiety Self-Help
Contains a variety of self-help methods for controlling anxiety attacks associated with Panic Disorder. The app includes articles about cognitive behavioural therapy (CBT), an anxiety diary and relaxation audio content. The developer, Excel At Life, produces a useful range of self-help apps relating to other stress disorders, including **Irrational Thinking CBT Test**, **Depression CBT Self-Help Guide** and more.

Diet

Ultimate Weight Watcher Diary
All-in-one tool for anyone trying to eat well or follow a weight-loss program, combining a daily food and exercise calculator, meal planner and weight tracker. A built-in barcode scanner lets you scan items to get instant nutritional details and add them in their entirety or by portion to your daily allowance calculation. A built-in database of thousands

of common items and chain restaurant menus means you can use the app in the supermarket or restaurant without need for an Internet connection. For a free alternative, try **Calorie Counter by FatSecret**. US users can also check out **Fooducate** for nutritional information of barcoded goods.

Noom Weight Loss Coach

From the makers of CardioTrainer, Noom helps you set up a personalized weight-loss plan, then sets you daily exercise and dietary tasks, monitors your progress and gives you a daily score.

Other health apps

Home Remedies

Nicely presented guide to natural remedies and complementary medicines for common ailments.

Water Your Body

Reminds you to drink water and keeps track of whether you're drinking enough throughout the day. For a no-frills, straightforward reminder, try **Drinking Water**.

QuitNow! Pro

Trying to give up smoking? This app will help keep you motivated, with tips, facts and advice. It'll also keep track of your days without smoking, calculating how much money and time you've saved and unlocking achievements to share with your friends. For more help giving up, try **Easy Stop Smoking** from Hypnotherapist Direct, one of the many self-hypnosis apps they offer.

Internet
Furrowed browsers

It sometimes seems as if half the apps out there are simply glorified interfaces for existing web content, replacing your need for a web browser in order to access your most visited sites. When you do need one, the stock Android™ browser does a great job, but there are some stellar alternatives well worth considering.

 ### Dolphin Browser HD

A lightning-fast, heavily featured web browser. It supports add-ons (with more than sixty currently available) and themes, multi-touch pinch zoom, tabbed browsing, RSS feeds, speed-dial, bookmark sorting and sync with Google™ Bookmarks, a customizable menu bar and full-screen mode. It also sports a password manager and assignable gesture commands.

Chrome Beta

Android 4.0 users can now try out this pre-release version of Google's popular web browser (it may be out of beta and/or available for older releases by the time you read this). It looks promising, with a slick user interface, tabs, incognito mode, bookmark sync, HTML5 support and more.

Opera Mini

Lightweight browser that compresses web sites before they reach you, meaning it can load pages faster and use less data – ideal for browsing on a limited data plan. It also syncs bookmarks with Opera on your desktop computer. A more fleshed-out release, **Opera Mobile**, is also available, or for another snappy, resource-light number, try **Miren Browser**.

Firefox

Seems a little on the heavy side for a mobile browser (it rolls in at 15MB), but it's worth a look if you use Firefox on your desktop and need bookmark, tabs, history and password sync, or fully realized add-on support. Tablet users will also appreciate its new tablet-optimized layout.

Skyfire

Enables you to watch Flash video content online by transcoding it into HTML5 on Skyfire's servers (free for three days, after which you'll need to purchase the video license fee). It also has some unique social networking integration, with built-in "like" buttons, a feed reader and "related ideas" search.

Kids
Baby and toddler apps

Whatever age your kids are, you'll find something to keep them busy and entertained right here. If you're installing an ad-supported free app, run it yourself for a while to see what kind of content is being advertised, as some third-party advertisers don't always flag ads of an adult nature. Developers are often unaware of this but usually quick to respond once alerted. If you like an app but don't trust the ads, an ad-free version is usually available for a small fee.

Babies

Baby Monitor & Alarm

Not a baby monitor in the conventional sense; you leave your Android™ device in your baby's room and it monitors sound levels, calling you on your chosen phone number if it detects any disturbance. The app can also be set to play lullabies, a recording of your own voice, or any tracks from your music library when triggered. Plus it keeps a log of activity through the night, so you can monitor sleep patterns and even replay any noises that were made.

Sleepy Baby

Turns your phone or tablet into a baby mobile and noise-maker, playing lullabies, nature sounds or white noise alongside soothing animations to gently light up a dark room and help your child fall alseep.

Toddlers

Toddler Lock

Child-friendly lock screen, allowing your toddler to doodle colourful shapes on your phone or tablet without accidentally opening other apps or making calls. For an alternative, try **Touch Born Paint Free Infant**.

Kid Mode

More sandboxed fun for your little ones, this offers a drawing and painting studio, storybooks and educational games and videos all in the same app. You can also enable other apps and games to be accessed from within Kid Mode, and a child lock prevents the app being exited by

accident, so you can focus elsewhere while your kid plays. For more, try **Famigo Sandbox**.

Whiz Kid

Beautiful puzzle game, with conundrums involving numbers, clocks, the alphabet, hidden objects, spot the difference and more. An entertaining way to help your child develop their arithmetic, problem solving, observational and logical thinking skills. Ads can (and probably should) be removed and new levels opened by purchasing an unlock code.

Kids Numbers and Math

One from an excellent range of pre-school learning apps from Intellijoy (other titles cover ABCs, reading, puzzles, colours and more). This absorbing game with friendly, colourful graphics will help your kid develop their basic maths skills – adding, subtracting and comparing numbers – with just enough fun to keep them entertained. For more learning games, try **Monkey Preschool Lunchbox**.

Animal Puzzle For Toddlers

Based on the wooden puzzles you used to get at play school – slot the animals into the correct-shaped holes. Simple, effective and charmingly rendered.

The Cat in the Hat – Dr. Seuss

Just one from a range of wonderful digital adaptations of classic children's books by Oceanhouse Media, with narration and sound effects to accompany the pages as they zoom and pan around the screen. Individual words are highlighted as the story is read, or when the corresponding part of the picture is touched. An engaging interactive book that your kids will want to read again and again. For more high-quality interactive books, take a look at the free titles offered by PlayTales.

Creativity

How to make Paper Airplanes

Clear, simple instructions for making a variety of paper aeroplanes. Folding diagrams can sometimes be a little hard to decipher, but this app includes helpful 3D animations to take the ambiguity out of all those dotted lines and bendy arrows. Should keep them quiet for an hour or two, at least till someone gets one in the eye.

Aircraft Carrier (12 steps)

Begin

PicsArt Goo – Liquid Face

PicsArt make a host of neat little Photoshop-like art toys, from their full-featured image editor (just called **PicsArt**, also available in a **For Kids** version) to fun distractions like **PicsArt Kaleidoscope** and this little gem, which lets you stretch, pinch and warp your photos. For more photo trickery, try **Camera Fun**.

Kids Doodle

Finger-doodle with a selection of brushes and effects (including neon and rainbow) which change randomly as you go. Sit back and watch as the app magically re-draws your picture in movie mode. For an app giving direct control over brush size and type, try **Paint Joy**.

Ethereal Dialpad

Not really a kids' app, but this easy-to-use synthesizer lets you play theremin-style by moving your finger around the screen, with very pleasing results. Intuitive enough to be able to pick up and use straight away, while easy enough on the ear not to get parents reaching for a hammer. For a more conventional selection of sounds, look for **Kids Musical Toy Set** or **Youth Musical Instruments**.

Games

FishFarts Kids

Frantic fish-farting fun. Tap on the fish as they swim by and they squeeze out an amusing fart noise and speed off leaving a trail of bubbles behind them. The kids version is free, a live wallpaper also available and a full game version can be procured for 61p. For more (admittedly, a bit weird) fart action, try **Poopee Animals** (p.168).

Ant Smasher

Addictive ant annihilation! This compelling game has a simple premise: squash the ants but don't touch the bees. For more oddly satisfying destroy-this-thing-while-avoiding-this-other-thing action, grab a copy of **Fruit Ninja**.

Tiny Tower

Absorbing little game where you build a tower block. You then assign the cute, pixel-faced tenants jobs in the restaurants and shops on each floor, making sure they're happy and that the shelves are well stocked.

Kids Socks

Possibly the most intense colour scheme ever seen in an app, this simple game requires you to find the matching socks and pants as they whizz along the washing line. Beautiful and incredibly vivid.

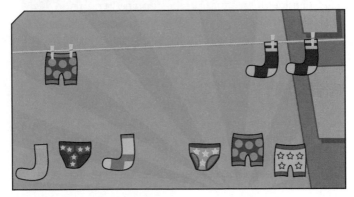

Lifestyle
Passing the time of day

Lifestyles, eh? We've all got one. Whatever you do with yours, there's almost certainly an app to help you do it.

Transparent Screen

If you like walking around but also like messing with your phone, you may well have found your attempts to combine the two activities to be slightly hazardous. Until now, that is. This app uses your device's camera to make your screen "transparent", showing you what's directly in front of you as you type and swipe. Say goodbye to falling down endless flights of stairs, slipping on banana skins or stepping in dog poo. Also ideal for using your phone while at the movies, a rock concert or theatre performance, in church, while operating heavy machinery or while using your other phone or tablet.

PaperKarma

Save the planet from the comfort of your own doormat. If you're in the US, you can use this app to unsubscribe from junk mail, by simply taking photos of offending items. PaperKarma figures out who's been sending you unsolicited mail and removes you from their list.

Speaktoit Assistant

Google Play™ is gradually becoming overpopulated with personal assistant apps. Most of them simply provide a friendly interface for your device's built-in speech recognition, but how well they can interpret and act on what you're asking them to do varies considerably. Speaktoit Assistant is the best all-rounder in our opinion: able to understand a broader

range of commands and access a broader range of applications in order to accomplish its tasks, including answering questions and performing searches, opening apps, sending messages and creating calendar entries. Competition is fierce in this area; it's also worth trying **Vlingo** and **Iris** to see which one works best for you.

Magic Mirror, Hair styler

Sick of seeing that same boring old barnet plonked on top of your head every time you look in the mirror? Maybe it's time for a change; this app lets you try out new hairstyles and colours on a photo of yourself. The results, to be honest, look a bit silly, but it's a fun way to realize your current mop doesn't look so bad after all.

 ## My Fashion Assistant

Closet organizer that lets you snap photos of your clothes or add in their pictures from online catalogues, and then mix and match them into outfits with a handy three-panel swipe-screen. Once in your inventory, clothes can be searched by colour, season or label. The app also lets you keep track of your favourite outfits, and when you last wore an item, so you can avoid the mortifying horror of people knowing you have a finite wardrobe.

 ## Entity Sensor Pro – EMF Detector

Uses your phone's magnetic sensor to detect fluctuations in the surrounding electromagnetic field. This could be irrefutable proof of a ghost breathing down your neck, or it could be the motor in your fridge playing up. Only you can know for sure. For more spectral speculation, try **Ghost EVP Analyzer**.

 ## MyDecision

Hmm, should I use the candlestick, the rope or the lead piping? When you're trying to make a complex decision based on a number of factors, this app will help you list your criteria and assign a value to each in terms of importance. It'll then spew out charts and graphs by rank so that you can see what your best option really is. For a quicker, more rudimentary pros-and-cons approach, try **Mobile Decision**. Now, which one should you try first?

Before I Die

Make a list of all those crazy, crazy things you want to do before you die but are either too inhibited, or poor, or busy just getting by to undertake. The app comes pre-loaded with a few to get you started, many of which you may have already done. The remainder will make excellent source material for something to whinge remorsefully about from your death bed.

Schemer

Another way to catalogue your pipe dreams. List the things you want to do and get advice and comments from people who've already done it. Part bucket list and part social network, Google Schemer™ is currently invite-only, but may well have become a full-blown release by the time you read this book.

Habit Streak Pro

Whether you're trying to eradicate a bad habit or cultivate a good one (sadly, the app won't tell you which is which), you can use Habit Streak to set goals or resolutions and track your progress over time. Did you just roll your eyes at me? Okay, that's going on your list.

Horoscope

Today's prediction: You will read a fascinating book written by a tall, dark stranger. This stranger will help you make difficult decisions relating to a piece of technology. He will show you an app that lets you read your horoscope by day, week, month or even year. Immediately after doing this, he will show you an app that gives you tarot readings.

Galaxy Tarot

Reads your tarot in a variety of card spreads, from drawing a single card to analysing a full spread for a professional reading. You can use the built-in tarot encyclopedia to browse the complete deck and better understand the various elements on each card and how one relates to another. Other features include a journal and a tarot card-of-the-day widget.

Family

Life360 Family Locator

Family tracker and locator service which uses GPS, Wi-Fi and cell triangulation to keep track of your loved ones' movements in and around disaster areas, or bad neighbourhoods (including your own), and whether they're safe or need help. It's also compatible with regular old mobile phones (for a monthly fee) so you can locate family members who don't have smartphones. Facilities include family chat, a one-touch check-in to let everyone know you're okay, and a panic alarm to let them know you're not.

Cozi Family Organizer

Shared family organizer, with a calendar, shopping lists, chore lists, a family journal and more. Cozi is also available for iPhones and BlackBerry phones, and from a web browser at cozi.com. Everyone in your family can share the same account, so you can make sure the occupants of your busy household are all on the same page.

Ancestry

Well-made family tree builder. You can start one from scratch in-app for free or continue work on an existing Ancestry.com entry while out researching. An essential tool for anyone serious about tracing their heritage.

Movies and video

Playing on the small screen

Whether you're a filmmaker, a movie buff or a couch potato, there's an app buried somewhere in here with your name on it.

Media players

MX Video Player

There are some exceptional video players on Google Play™, and MX Video Player is one of the best available, happily playing almost any video and subtitle format beautifully. Under the hood it supports multi-core decoding (taking full advantage of your device's dual-core CPU) with highly optimized codecs and renderers. You can swipe left to right for forward and rewind and pinch to zoom in and out, while the edges of the screen control brightness and volume. For some great alternatives, try **MoboPlayer** or **Rock Player**.

Plex

Plex is a media player that works in conjunction with Plex media server for Mac or PC (available for free from plexapp.com) to easily browse and stream movies, photos and music directly from your computer to your Android™ device.

myPlayer

If you don't have Flash installed on your device, you can use this app to stream media from the BBC's iPlayer service to your Android device. It can also stream live TV and radio from other sources, and streaming can be set to low quality for use over a 3G connection. Arguably better than the BBC's own iPlayer app (also available from Google Play).

Netflix

Subscription to Netflix lets you use this app to stream TV episodes and movies to your Android device. The selection is as comprehensive as any of those offered by the big DVD rental services, and you can even start watching on your Android and continue where you left off on your TV or computer (or vice-versa). For a free alternative (but obviously

with much less choice over what you watch), check out **Crackle** or **MovieVault**.

JetflicksTV

Subscription-based service offering ad-free HD-quality movies and TV streamed to your phone or tablet. The selection of titles available is decent, and listings are updated daily, so you can catch the latest episodes of your favourite shows as they become available. For more TV on the go, try **TV.com**.

Remote Control

Gmote 2.0

Turns your phone or tablet into a Wi-Fi remote control for your computer's media player. Once you've installed the Gmote server program on your computer, setup is simple, and you'll be able to browse and launch any media. It also lets you stream media wirelessly to your Android™ device, and can act as a wireless keyboard and mouse.

Unified Remote

Like Gmote, this app will turn your Android device into a media controller, keyboard and mouse for your Windows PC. The basic version has most of the common requirements covered, while the full version of the app includes more specific integration with a range of popular media players (Boxee, Hulu, iTunes, MediaMonkey, Netflix, Pandora, Spotify, VLC, XMBC and more) and web browsers (Firefox, Chrome, Opera and Internet Explorer).

Reference

Movies by Flixster

A moviegoer's toolkit. Gives you instant access to a vast database of movie reviews, trailers and information from Rotten Tomatoes. You can get local cinema listings with show times and find nearby restaurants on a Google Map™, watch trailers, share your own ratings with Facebook friends, manage your Netflix queue and more.

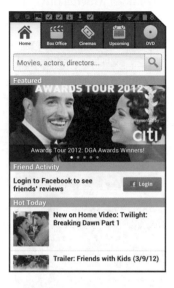

IMDb

Access IMDb's database of over a million movies and TV shows with a few taps of your screen. You can read reviews, view trailers, check local screening times, get the latest entertainment news, look up TV episode recaps and more. You can also flag individual movies or actors for notifications of any new activity, and scan DVD covers or barcodes for instant movie details.

Mizuu

Pulls together your digital movie collection into an exquisitely displayed database, including summaries, actor information, trailers and posters from IMDb. Mizuu isn't a media player itself, but it's a neat way to organize and browse your collection. For more, try **My Movies**.

RunPee

Nature can call at some of the most inopportune moments: in the middle of a movie, for example. But when you've got to go, you've got to go. What happens if you miss something important? Fear not, this handy little app will tell you the best time to run out of the cinema to relieve yourself during a lull in the action. For those of you who like to turn up late at a movie showing, it'll also fill you in with a synopsis of the first five minutes you just missed. It won't, however, apologize to everyone whose legs you stumble over on the way to your seat.

Making your own

Movie Studio

The best app currently available for editing video is Google™ Movie Studio. It lets you trim individual clips, splice them together, add soundtracks and upload to YouTube™. Movie Studio isn't available from Google Play™, but

comes pre-installed on some more recent Android™ phones and tablets. If your device doesn't have it, you could do worse than do a quick web search for "Google Movie Studio .apk" and see if you can find a download. If it's just simple trimming of individual movie clips you need, check out **VidTrim**.

Clesh

If you can't lay your hands on a copy of Movie Studio, or it isn't compatible with your device, try this. Its editing facilities are actually pretty good, but the app requires to you upload all your raw material to the cloud before you can start working – and with video files this can be both time- and bandwidth-consuming.

Qik Video Lite

Set yourself up with a free account at qik.com, install the app, and you'll be able to broadcast live streaming Internet video over Wi-Fi in real time to the world (or, if you prefer, just to your chosen few). Qik also supports live sharing to Facebook, Twitter and other sites. A premium subscription gives you HD and 3D recording, video chat and video mail, and unlimited video archive storage for sharing later.

Clayframes

Lets you make stop-motion animation and time-lapse movies. Useful features include the ability to trigger the camera shutter by clapping your hands, onion skinning (image overlay) to help make animations smooth, and timed shutter release. For an alternative, try **Stop-Motion**, or for simple time-lapse filming, try **Time-Lapse**.

Videocam Illusion Pro

Video camera replacement that adds filters and effects in real time as you film. The effects on offer are pretty good for messing around with, encompassing colour and blur filters and old camera simulators, image distortions, blurring, mirroring, and special effects such as ascii art, x-ray, negative, chalk and more.

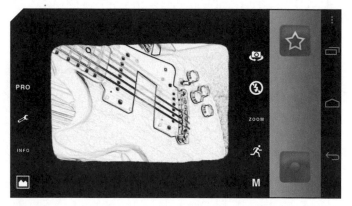

Music
Listening pleasure

Whether you're into streaming, radio or listening to your existing collection, there's no shortage of apps to help you get the most out of your music.

Music players

Google Play™ Music

Google™'s own **Music** app will probably have shipped with your device. It's a decent, straightforward MP3 player with most of the basic functions you're likely to need. Where it really shines (for US users, at least) is its ability to hook up with the music section of Google Play™, enabling you to buy new music straight from the app. You can also use Google's Music Manager desktop program on your computer to upload your entire collection to the cloud (currently you can store twenty thousand songs for free) and stream to all your Android™ devices over Wi-Fi or 3G/4G. US users can get a similar service from the **Amazon MP3** app, which allows you to stream music from your Amazon Cloud Drive.

DoubleTwist

A media player for both your Android device and desktop computer. Once installed on both, you can

use it to sync music, videos, photos and podcasts from one device to the other over USB (and wirelessly when used with the **AirSync** plugin). The desktop player has Amazon's MP3 store built in, giving the whole set up a very iTunes-like feel for buying and syncing music. It also has a facility for subscribing to podcasts. Meanwhile, the Android app provides a solid, all-round media player, with music, video and podcasts all covered. It has a streaming radio player, too, with hundreds of stations browsable by category. DoubleTwist is definitely a step up from Android's stock Music app, with rating support, and some nice navigation features like swiping to skip forward and back. Add in desktop sync and optional (rather expensive) add-ons, including automated album-art downloading, and it's tough to beat.

WinAmp

Another full-featured music player, WinAmp has the edge over DoubleTwist in that its long-standing desktop program is as good a media player as you're likely to find. Run both together and get wireless syncing for free.

PowerAmp

Very powerful, dedicated music player. For playing locally stored files (streaming isn't supported) it's one of the best out there. It has an unparalleled ten-band equalizer and tone controls, built-in album art finder and MP3 tag editor, cross-fade and gapless playback support, lyrics support (with lyrics search), lock screen controls and an excellent set of widgets and themes.

It handles most music file types, including MP3, MP4/M4A, alac, ogg, wma, flac, wav and ape, and supports scrobbling your listens to Last.fm. Similar features can also be found in **Player Pro**.

 iSyncr

Devout iTunes users, this is your best solution for syncing your Android device with your iTunes playlist, complete with album art, ratings, play counts and other statistics. Now you can finally send that old iPod off to get recycled back into water pistols and Christmas cracker puzzles.

Saving screenshot...

Listening...

Discovery

Shazam/
Encore

Hey, what's that song they're playing on the radio? Point your phone's mic in the direction of the music and **Shazam** will listen to it for a few seconds and get back to you with the answer. It'll also provide lyrics and discographies, grab tour dates and link up with Amazon, Spotify, YouTube™ and other services to let you buy, listen or watch at your convenience. It's pretty acccurate for straightforward, melodic material, but the more wayward your tastes are, the less luck you're likely to have with it. If Shazam isn't quite doing it for you, try **SoundHound**.

Last.fm

Pick an artist or genre and this app will build a playlist for you and stream it to your phone. Last.fm also "scrobbles" your music listening habits from your media player, uploading play counts to your page online and feeding you similar artists and recommendations. Tracks link up to an encyclopedia of information about each artist. Part-social network app, it also lets you view the details and stats of other users with similar tastes.

Campscout

Lets you search, play and buy music direct from independent artists (in just about any format you could possibly want) at Bandcamp.com. That's pretty much all it does, but it does it incredibly well. For a more Spotify-like approach to Bandcamp's content, try **Bandroid for Bandcamp**.

MP3 Music Download Pro

Search for and download MP3s, album art and lyrics by almost any artist, for free.

Gigbox

Love live music? Gigbox gives you a heads up when your favourite bands are playing in town. You can also search for gigs by location (globally), venue or artist, add events to your calendar, buy tickets and get directions on a map.

At the gig, the app enters Live mode, enabling you to chat with other audience members and publish pictures and ratings to mygigbox.com from your phone. For more live music listings, try **GigBeat**.

Radio & streaming

TuneIn Radio/Pro

Offers more than fifty thousand local and international radio stations and 1.2 million Internet streams. Ideal for finding new stations or taking your favourite ones with you when travelling. The Pro version also lets you record streams to your device's SD card. For an alternative, try **Stitcher Radio**.

Spotify

In case you hadn't noticed, the Internet is spilling over with subscription-based music streaming services. Pay a monthly fee and get instant access to millions upon millions of tracks anywhere, to stream or listen to offline. The Spotify app gives you 48 hours free access to their premium service so that you can check out what all the fuss is about.

Pandora

Inhabitants of the US can install the Pandora app and have personalized content streamed to their Android™ devices. Start off with the name of a favourite artist or song and let Pandora create a 'station' for you, consisting of similar content. For more streamed music, try **Rdio** or **8tracks**.

Instruments & recording

Cleartune – Chromatic Tuner

If tuners came in tins, this one would do exactly what it says on the tin. It's a charming-looking, responsive chromatic tuner you can use to tune any instrument that makes a sound. For a good free alternative try **DaTuner Free** or **gStrings Free**.

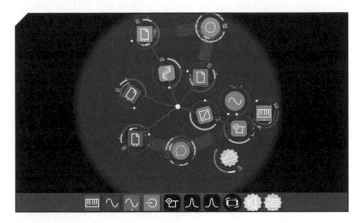

Reactable mobile
Versatile, fun and very playable modular synthesizer based on the award-winning instrument used by Björk on recent tours. It works by selecting and placing modules (synths, sample, effects, loops, direct sound input and more) onto the circular instrument and rotating, linking and moving them to adjust their sound. For more touchscreen synth action, check out **Plasma Sound**, **Pulsate** and **NodeBeat**.

My Guitar
Musical apps on Android™ are one of the areas where the platform still lags (literally) behind iOS. It seems difficult for developers to build virtual instruments that are as playable and responsive as their iPhone equivalents. My Guitar

comes close, but is still a little "laggy" even on an up-to-date device. It requires you to fret the strings with one hand while strumming with the other. Support for bending and muting of strings makes this feel more like a real guitar than some other apps do, but can make it hard to master. For a more immediately playable but ultimately limited instrument, try **Solo**.

Piano For You

Best of a bunch of piano apps, this one is responsive, has decent sounds and a scrollable full-length split-level keyboard. The full version also includes an accordion, organ and electric piano. You could also try **My Piano**, from the same developer as My Guitar, which has a nice variety of sounds and effects to choose from, but only a single or double octave keyboard from which to operate.

Caustic 2

An electronic studio in your pocket. Caustic combines drum machines, synths, effects, a sequencer and a mixer into one app. Naturally it's geared towards making dance and electronic music, but the range of sounds is fairly versatile and it's fun to dabble with even if your tastes lie elsewhere. It's also worth taking a look at **Audiotool Sketch** and **PocketBand Uloops**. For multitrack live instrument recording, try **J4T**.

Hi-Q MP3 Recorder

Simple one-track recorder offering a vast improvement over the stock app that shipped with your phone or tablet. Ideal for dictation, recording practices and concerts, and more. For even better quality with uncompressesd audio (but larger file sizes), try **PCM Recorder**.

News and magazines

Read all about it

Websites and blogs often add new content as they publish it to a "feed" that you can subscribe to. A news reader or aggregator will collect these new articles so you can read them all from one app without having to trudge round the same old sites every day. Podcatchers operate in a similar way for podcasts, routinely checking for new episodes and downloading them for listening (or watching) at your convenience.

Google Reader

A simple but effective free app for aggregating web content. It syncs with a Google Reader™ account for easy subscribing to newsfeeds from a web browser. You can also use it to manage any podcasts you're subscribed to with Google Listen™. Google Reader accounts can also be accessed by a number of third-party reader apps, prime examples being **Pulse** (below), **gReader** and **NewsRob**, or for tablets, **Newsr** and **JustReader News**.

Pulse

Pulse lets you set up RSS feeds to your favourite sources and stores them for you in a friendly, scrollable grid format that looks great on a phone and even better on a tablet. Setting up pages for different kinds of content and managing feeds is a doddle. It'll even pull in content from your social networks, allowing you to wallow through your morning coffee/Facebook/news ritual all from the same location. It syncs with a Google Reader account, if you use one. If you sign up for a free pulse.me account you can also sync with Read It Later, Instapaper and other services. For a similar magazine-style approach to newsfeeds, try **SkyGrid** or **Feedly**.

News360

News aggregator pulling in content from over ten thousand sources around the globe. You can tailor your news stream to your interests, save stories for offline reading and get local stories based on GPS location. If you're the kind of person who doesn't mind handing over access to your other online accounts, it'll even take your Facebook, Twitter, Evernote and Google+™ content and automatically personalize your newsfeed.

Google
Currents
New (at time of
writing US only) service
serving up free content from
publishers such as Forbes,
Techcrunch, Popular Science,
Saveur and many more.
Currents™ also integrates
with your Google Reader
subscriptions and presents
them in a beautiful magazine-
like format (some with video
and slideshows, live maps and
other multimedia content)
alongside "trending editions",
an hourly edition covering the
latest stories in a range of categories.

 FlyScreen
FlyScreen pulls in RSS news content, Facebook and
Twitter updates, weather and other web content
and displays it all on your lock screen. About as close as you
can get to keeping your finger on the pulse without actually
having to move your fingers much. For similar features in a
home screen widget, try **Minimal Reader**.

 Read It Later
Lets you save web articles and videos for offline
viewing, removing unnecessary images and

formatting. Available for all mobile platforms and as add-ons for Chrome and Firefox, it lets you save items from your desktop or any other device and have them sync automatically with your phone or tablet. Perfect for loading your phone up with reading matter before heading off on a commute.

DoggCatcher

Everything you need in a podcatcher, DoggCatcher manages podcasts (both audio and video) and newsfeeds. It supports automated downloads and deletion of played files, playlists, variable playback speed (with the **Presto** add-on), and playback position recall. It comes with a huge library of feeds to peruse, and can provide recommendations based on your subscriptions. For a prettier interface in exchange for fewer high-end features, try **Pocket Casts** or **BeyondPod**.

StumbleUpon

Join the millions of other Stumblers as they stumble around. No, it's not a zombie flick, it's a social network thing based on sharing interesting content with like-minded people. Tap the "Stumble" button or just browse the recommendations to find new and unexpected content.

Juxtapoz Art & Culture Magazine | Feb-12

Zinio

Beautiful, easily navigable reader and store for digital magazines (some with exclusive multimedia content) from major publishers around the world. Buy single issues or take out a subscription and sync your collection with other devices. Read from the original full-colour layouts or in text-only mode. The app looks and feels amazing on both phones and tablets, and comes loaded with a selection of free editions covering a range of interests to get you started. For more digital zine content, take a look at **Issuu**.

Redditmag+

Reddit users, this app is a nifty way to browse reddit content visually. It collects images from reddit articles and presents them in a large, appealing grid, which can be filtered by category. Tap on an image to read the full article. For a more straightforward interface, try **Reddit News** or **Bacon Reader**.

Global News & Newspapers

Many publications these days provide apps which basically just pull in content from their own website. This app is one of many that aggregates links to news sites from all over the world and provides a useable front end for accessing all of them from one place. Publications are browsable by country or type, and making a selection simply takes you to the desired paper's web content via the app's internal browser. Of the many we tested, Global News & Newspapers has the biggest selection and allows you to add favourites and manually add links to sites not already present.

CitizenSide

Global photojournalism community that lets you see pictures and video from world events as they happen, unfiltered by the mainstream media. You can also share photos of your own; if you witness a newsworthy event and upload pictures, the service can act as an agent for licensing them around the world (you get up to 65 percent of any money earned), even sending you on local missions from international clients looking for content. For more user-submitted news content, try **Meporter**.

Personalization
Tweak for yourself

Almost every aspect of your Android™ device's look and feel can be customized to your needs, from simple tweaks like changing your icons and widgets, ringtones and wallpapers, to more complex stuff involving automations and behaviours. Advanced users can even "root" their devices, allowing them to install customized versions of the Android platform.

Google Gesture Search

Perform quick operations without having to browse through your phone's menus. Simply draw the first couple of letters of your required app or contact and a shortlist will appear. Gesture Search™ can be set up so you can trigger it with a simple flick of the wrist away from you and back.

Widgets & Wallpapers

Android Pro Widgets

Useful range of scalable, scrollable, themeable widgets, including calendar (including voice input), contacts, bookmarks, messaging, Facebook and Twitter (including update widgets), Timeline and other tools.

WidgetLocker

Lets you modify your lock screen with wallpapers, sliders for changing brightness and volume, and a whole host of other settings and customizations. You can place shortcuts, apps, control panels and any widgets you like for quick and easy access without having to unlock your device.

Beautiful Widgets

A nice selection of customizable widgets in various sizes, including clocks, switches and animated live weather. Widgets can be "skinned", with skins available to download from the app. Admittedly, most are pretty hideous, but there's enough good stuff in there to keep most happy. For more fancy stuff, try **HD Widgets** or **Fancy Widgets**. For a more minimal vibe, check out **Clean Widgets**.

Extended Controls

Like a power control widget on steroids, Extended Controls lets you create skinnable switch arrays for access to your device settings. In addition to screen brightness, GPS, Bluetooth and other standard toggles, you get over thirty more switches, including stay awake, flashlight, reboot, USB tether, Wi-Fi hotspot, volume controls, haptic feedback and more. It also includes clock, notifications and system-info widgets.

Wallpapers HD

Search for "wallpaper" on Google Play™ and you'll be eyeball-deep in mixed results. This app will help you get at least down to waist-deep in fairly decent results. As well as arranging backgrounds by category, the app also lets you search by colour, or even take a lucky dip.

Launchers

Launcher Pro

Smooth, fast launcher replacement. The interface is incredibly responsive and can really make an older device feel less laggy. It also supports up to seven home screens and has a smooth-scrolling 3D app drawer.

ADW Launcher

Another great, highly customizable launcher with an excellent selection of themes available. Supports shortcuts and folders, configurable swipe gestures and more.

Go Launcher EX

A great place to start if you're thinking of dipping your toe into the wonderful world of launchers. Go Launcher combines the best elements of most of the other heavy hitters, with widgets galore, thousands upon thousands of themes, delightful transition effects, and enough power

under the hood to keep you tweaking for weeks. The developers offer popular customizations for nearly every aspect of your phone: it's also worth checking out **Go Keyboard**, **Go Lock** and **Go SMS** for more interface enhancements.

 SPB Shell 3D
Offers a painfully slick 3D home screen with 3D widgets, and smooth 3D animated page transitions.

Keyboards

 Swype
Wonderful keyboard replacement that lets you input text rapidly by sliding between letters without taking your finger off the screen. The app is incredibly forgiving of sloppy input and remarkably seems to nearly always generate accurate type. To install it, direct your browser to swype.com and follow the

instructions. If swype isn't compatible with your device, try **SlideIt**, which offers a similar approach.

Swiftkey X

It may look just like any other keyboard, but SwiftkeyX has an impressive text prediction engine that seems to know what you're going to type next even before you do. Instead of just auto-completing each individual word as you type, it actually learns your writing habits and attempts to predict your next word, becoming increasingly accurate the more you use it. Simply hit the space bar to approve the suggested word, or tap one of the other suggestions either side. It can optionally monitor your Gmail™, Facebook and Twitter posts for greater accuracy.

8pen

Bizarre but strangely effective text interface (you can't really call it a keyboard in a conventional sense). It divides your type area into four zones and

divides letters up between them. A predictive text engine lets you enter text by tapping between the zones. Think of it as old-school mobile phone texting taken up another notch.

Hacker's Keyboard

Tablet users looking for an upgrade from the stock keyboard will find this a worthy replacement. It offers a full five-row keyboard, complete with Esc/Ctrl and arrow keys (supporting multi-touch for these and other modifier keys, such as Shift). It also supports multiple language keyboard layouts

Profiles & automation

Tasker

A powerhouse of an app that automates functions on your device, based on criteria like its location, the time of day, the phone's orientation and so on. As a battery-saving trick, for example, you could set Wi-Fi to stop when your screen switches off. Or minimize late-night disturbances by setting your phone to automatically go into silent mode between midnight and 8am, but only if your GPS location indicates that you're at home. Make a media player start up as soon as a cable is plugged into the headphone socket, switch your wallpaper from a picture of your cat to something more professional-looking when you arrive at work (a picture of your cat in a suit and tie, for example) and so on. It also works with plugins for the similarly versatile **Locale**. For a free alternative to see if this is your kind of thing, take a look at **AutomateIt**.

Setting Profiles Lite/Full

Like Tasker, this app will let you set your device to various different states based on location, time of day, battery power and a list of other criteria. It's a little simpler than Tasker and geared more towards saved profile states that can be triggered or switched manually. For more profile-oriented automation, try **PhoneWeaver**.

Sounds

Llama – Location Profiles

Lets you set up automated sound profiles based on your location or the time of day. Set your phone to vibrate or play a more conservative ringtone while at work, to silent at night, or anything you like. You can also set specific contacts to override other settings, so that you don't miss an important call. The app uses phone masts to determine your location, so there's no need to leave GPS switched on. For more sound-profile control, check out **Vibe** or **Soundify**.

Ringtone Maker Pro Free

Take complete control of all of your phone's ringtones and notification sounds. This app lets you pick any song or sound file currently stored on your device's SD card and quickly crop it down to the part you want to use. Edited sounds can be saved as ringtones, alarms, notification sounds or just a straightforward music clip.

Photography
Picture perfect

When you take into account its access to GPS coordinates, touch-screen interactivity, computing power and Internet connectivity, the little pinhole camera lens that peeks out from the back of your phone probably has more power within its potential grasp than your actual camera (image quality aside). Google Play™ hosts a staggering number of camera-related apps, all aiming to help you get the most out of that tiny, tiny lens.

Cameras

HDR Camera +

Takes amazing images using HDR (High Dynamic Range), a photographic technique where the same scene is shot several times over a range of exposures, which are then blended together to create a more intense, detailed image. Simply tap to take a picture; the app compensates for camera shake so there's no need for a tripod or unusually steady hand. It also de-ghosts any objects that may have moved during the multiple exposures. Photos are combined and tone-mapped into HDR images within a few seconds, and tone-mapping paremeters can be adjusted, giving you complete control over contrast, colour vividness and exposure.

Quickest Camera

For when you need to take a picture in a hurry and don't have time to open up your camera app, focus and shoot, in case you miss the action. Place this app on your home screen, and with a single tap it'll launch while instantaneously taking a snap.

3DSteroid Pro

Creates 3D stereoscopic images without the need for a 3D camera. Take a picture, move a little, and take another picture. The app lets you output your image in a variety of 3D formats, compatible with a range of 3D glasses (both the modern and old-fashioned red and blue kind), a cross-eyed version, and a rather pleasing "wiggle", which rapidly alternates between left and right views (great for making animated GIFs).

Pano

Take stunning, seamless panoramic photos. Pano doesn't take one continuous photo, like the Android™ 4.0 camera app can, but instead lets you take a series of pictures which it then knits together into one continuous image. A transparent overlay of your previous snap helps you keep things lined up in order to give the app a fighting chance. Once your shots are taken, they're aligned, blended and colour-adjusted into a breathtaking vista. For a more ICS-like continuous shot, try **360 – Create amazing panoramas**.

Effects & editors

Pixlr-o-matic

Offers a beautiful array of filters, lighting adjustments, retro and vintage effects, and custom frames and overlays which can be combined into over two million different combinations. It also offers a randomizer

mode to give your photos some added pizzazz with a single tap. Tweak images from your gallery or take snaps directly from the app's built-in camera. There are plenty of other photo effect suites out there to choose from, some excellent examples being **Camera 360**, **Camera Zoom FX**, **Little Photo** and **Vignette**.

TouchRetouch

Useful photo retouching app similar to Photoshop's Clone Stamp or Magic Healing Brush tools. Remove items from your photos by painting over or lassoing round them and tapping "Go'". The app grafts in adjacent parts of the image to make the offending objects vanish. Perfect for erasing your ex from holiday snaps, zits, scars, bruises and rogue hairs from your otherwise beautiful visage, and a whole heap of other selective memory enhancing uses.

Adobe Photoshop Touch

Tablet-only app that ports the most useful tools from the ubiquitous desktop image editor to a touch interface. As well as familiar features such as the clone stamp, blur tool, brushes and layers, Photoshop Touch adds a few tricks of its own, including filling part of a picture with other images captured with your camera, and selecting areas by scribbling on them. It also includes sophisticated and intuitive selection tools, integrated Google™ image search and more.

Comic Strip It! pro

Lets you arrange your photos into a comic strip, complete with a range of caption and speech bubble styles. Use existing images or take shots directly into

the app, and then rotate, scale and add effects and captions to each frame as required. As well as making comic strips, you could also use this app to make step-by-step instructions, storyboards, memes and more.

Galleries

QuickPic
This lightweight, simple image browser feels quite similar to the stock Android™ 4.0 gallery and offers most of the same functions, with the addition of being able to hide or password protect individual items.

JustPictures!
Image browser with excellent multi-service synchronization support. As well as browsing and editing locally stored images, the app lets you browse, search, download and upload to any accounts you have with Picasa™,

Flickr, Smugmug, Facebook, Photobucket, Windows Live, Tumblr, Deviant Art and Imgur, bringing all your photos together in one place.

Utilities

Photo Tools Pro

Everything the professional photographer needs in one place (apart from an actual camera and a way with animals and kids). Contains thirty tools, from timers, check lists and a notepad, to depth of field, exposure and bellows extension calculators, a light meter, colour temperature chart, weather forecast, EXIF reader and more.

Sun Surveyor

Predicts the position of the sun and moon based on GPS location, time and date. It includes a 3D compass, map view, and camera view with augmented reality overlay. An indispensible tool for photographers and filmmakers looking to predict the best times of day for shooting at a particular location, how long they have before the sun moves behind

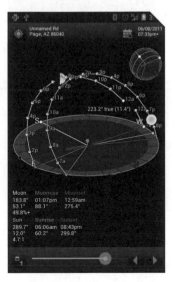

a building, when to shoot for golden hour and blue hour, shadow length and direction and more. For an alternative, take a look at **The Photographer's Ephemeris** or **LightTrac**.

PhotoCaddy – Photography Guide

Professional photography advice for fifty different situations, from portraits, animals and plants to fireworks, aerial and macro photography. Each subject provides suggested camera settings, tips (including user-submitted tips), and a place to keep notes of your own. For more photography tips and tricks, try **Photography Trainer**.

Photo Transfer App

Quick and easy way to transfer photos and videos between your PC, Mac, iPhone, iPad, or other Android™ devices over a Wi-Fi network. The app gives you a short address to key into a web browser and lets you move your files around from there. Alternately, you can transfer photos to your other devices automatically as they're taken by syncing with a **Dropbox** account (see p.121).

Productivity
Keeping busy

Your Android™ device can be a fantastic tool to help you stay productive when away from your desk. With to-do lists, note-keeping apps and a whole host of creative utilities, you'll never have to waste time relaxing and having fun ever again.

Pomodroido

A simple, straightforward timer for using the Pomodoro technique – a basic productivity technique where you work for 25 minutes on your given task, then take a break for five minutes, then work again for another 25. It's a great way to break up your workload into digestible chunks and set incremental deadlines. After four work sessions, you can take a fifteen-minute break

– you've earned it. The app also provides little productivity tips on screen, and integration with Astrid task lists is promised for a future release. Durations for work and rest periods are all adjustable, as are notification sounds and ticking (which can thankfully be switched off). Looking for a straightforward timer? Check out **Ultimate Stopwatch** or **Timer**.

Stop Procrastination

A self-hypnosis audio app to help you stay focused and stop procrastinating. Install it right now! Oh, hang on, read the rest of this chapter first.

DroidEdit Pro (code editor)

If you're not a web developer, you can go and make a cup of tea for the duration of this review. This text-based source-code editor supports syntax highlighting for C, C++, C#, Java, HTML, CSS, Python, SQL and a few other commonly used languages, search and replace, alternate character encodings, and has a useful arsenal of keyboard shortcuts, accessible either from an external keyboard, or from a virtual keyboard replacement such as **Hacker's Keyboard** (p.105). Okay, the rest of you can come back in now.

µTorrent Remote

Works with µTorrent for Windows and Mac, letting you make a secure connection to your desktop to remotely start, stop and check progress on your uploads and downloads from any Internet connection. You can also remotely add new torrents, and have completed ones sent to your phone for use. For a fully operational torrent client, try **tTorrent** (p.147), or the Android release of **µTorrent** itself, which is currently in development and should be available by the time you read this.

PdaNet

If your device doesn't have a USB tether facility enabled you can use this app to share your mobile Internet connection with your PC or Mac. Also useful for providing a Wi-Fi connection for an old laptop. The app comes bundled with **SMS Agent**, which lets you send and receive text messages from your computer.

Ubuntu for Android

Still currently in development, the popular Linux-based OS will soon be available for Android devices. It runs in parallel with your Android system, enabling you to connect your device to a keyboard, mouse and monitor (or HDTV) and use it as a full desktop PC that you can carry around in your pocket. Check ubuntu.com/devices/android for more details.

To-do lists

Astrid Tasks

To-do lists aren't exactly the most exciting thing on the planet, although it does depend somewhat on what you've got on your list. If yours is full of all the nasty stuff that you just wouldn't get on with unless there was either a really big carrot or a really big stick in the vicinity, you're not alone. Astrid is an encouraging little pink octopus thing that arranges your to-dos and sends you quirky little reminders, usually more carrot than stick: "A little snack after you finish this?", or "Ready to put this behind you?". Behind the cute facade, Astrid is a masterful taskmaster, syncing with Google Tasks™, Producteev and Astrid.com. It supports multiple lists and list sharing, and a handful of paid-for plugins, allowing you to add tasks via voice, trigger reminders based on location and more. For a less quirky multi-syncing task manager, try **Wunderlist**.

Any.DO

Intuitive, gesture-controlled to-do list. Any.DO supports voice input, can automatically add contact links to tasks based on any names that crop up in your task description, syncs with Google Tasks (with more services to be added in future versions) and supports shared tasks with notifications and reminders. Managing your list is as easy as drag-and-dropping to rearrange them, and swiping completed items to cross them out. Completed tasks can be removed from the list by shaking your device. The app's clean, spacious interface is a joy to use, one of the nicest in any of the vast number of to-do lists available.

Notes & ideas

Evernote

Evernote looks like a humble note-taking service, but beneath its surface lies a powerful web-based capture tool. Register for a free account at evernote.com and the app will let you send text and audio notes to yourself, upload photos, scanned text and other files, tag them and access them from anywhere via your web browser. Any writing in images you upload gets transcribed into searchable text. It's a neat way to keep all your ideas, reminders and notes in one place. It integrates with free desktop apps for PC and Mac and there's also a paid account option offering more storage space. If you use both Google Calendar™ and Evernote, try **Meshin Recall**, which lets you combine the two services and add Evernote items to your calendar events.

Springpad

Another well-rounded cloud-based note-taking service. Kind of an automated scrapbook where you can dump all of your ideas, barcode-scanned products, web links, photos, snippets, recipes, voice memos and more.

Send them all to Springpad and have them automatically categorized and synced. You can add tags and separate items into project folders. A worthy competitor to Evernote.

Groovy Notes for Tablets

Nicely designed personal organizer-styled tool for taking memos and audio notes, all tagged by date and fully searchable. A few features feel like they still need a bit of fine-tuning, but in terms of user interface, this app presents some serious eye candy, and sometimes it's better to have an app that just makes you want to use it than one that's ruthlessly efficient. Definitely one to watch. For more luxurious style-over-content journal keeping, try **Beautiful Notes**.

Classic notes + App Box

On the surface this looks like a rudimentary notepad app, but it comes with a smorgasbord of powerful features and tiny, useful utilities including audio notes and voice memos, image support, lockable private notes, video notes, paint notes, attachments, status bar, Google Translate™, Google Docs™ and Google Calendar™ integration, to-do list, reminders, tagging, colour-coding, searching and sorting, a dictionary and thesaurus, postcode lookup, stopwatch, unit converter and much, much more.

Tape-a-Talk Voice Recorder

Compact, high-quality voice recorder supporting wav and 3gp file formats in a range of qualities up to 16-bit 44kHz (CD quality). The Pro version includes fast forward and rewind facilities, and a widget for instant record.

Sync

Dropbox

A free service that syncs your stuff among all of your devices. Just drag an item into your dropbox and it'll upload in the background, automatically saving to your other devices and to Dropbox's own servers. You get 2GB free cloud storage, with more available by referring friends, and (currently) by letting the app auto-upload photos and videos from your device's camera. A painless way to wirelessly transfer files and keep backups. For a great alternative Dropbox client, try **Dropsync**.

FolderSync

Simple, but powerful, FolderSync provides two-way sync between your Android™ and multiple cloud storage accounts, including SkyDrive, Dropbox, SugarSync, Ubuntu One, Box.net, LiveDrive, HiDrive, NetDocuments, Amazon S3 and FTP. You get full control of which folders sync with which services, and Tasker and Locale support lets you automate syncing based on various criteria. As if that weren't enough, the app is also a fully fledged file manager. For simple wireless syncing between devices via a web browser, try **Cheetah Sync** or **WiFi File Explorer** (p.148).

Creativity

 Autodesk Sketchbook Mobile

Truly a professional grade painting and drawing app, Sketchbook Mobile opens up with an innocent-looking blank canvas, but as soon as you start using it, it becomes apparent that this is no toy. You get a useful, fully editable set of brushes, pencils, air brushes, marker pens and more, an intuitive, well thought-out interface with an easy-to-use colour picker, and the most important brush controls (size and opacity) are editable with a simple vertical or horizontal swipe gesture. You also get hi-res output to JPEG, PNG or PSD, multiple layers and a whole heap of other pro features.

Tablet users should check out Autodesk's **Sketchbook Pro**, which offers a similar feature set with a tablet-optimized interface. A cheaper, slightly more nimble sketchbook program can be found in the form of **Fresco Pro**.

 Adobe Touch suite

Adobe, makers of the ubiquitous Photoshop, provide this suite of tablet-oriented touchscreen apps aimed at creative types. The apps are $9.99 each and include **Collage**, for assembling mood boards combining drawing, images and text; **Kuler**, for generating harmonious colour themes; **Ideas**, a vector-based digital sketchpad; **Proto**, for building wireframe prototype website designs; and **Photoshop Touch** (see p.111). The individual apps have some good features and some frustrating omissions (no layers available in **Ideas**, for example, nor can it export to EPS or Adobe Illustrator formats) that may have more demanding users pulling their hair out. But for certain uses, some of these apps are currently the best or only tools available for the Android™ platform.

Mindjet

Makes it easy to construct mind maps – a way to organize information into branches, nodes and subnodes. You can add attachments and links, customize styles and colours, tag and sort by keywords. The interface lets you drag and drop, zoom, and perform common commands with gesture or keyboard shortcuts. For a similarly powerful app with a less conventional, hand-drawn look, try **Mindboard**.

Security and privacy

Playing it safe

The number of Android™ devices in use is on the up, and wherever there are people using a service, there will always be a contingent looking for new ways to exploit them. From software risks in the form of malware and malicious apps to the practical risks posed by loss or theft of a portable device containing sensitive personal data, it only takes a few simple measures to keep yourself protected.

Passwords & locks

 ### Void Lock

A crafty lock screen that makes it appear as if your phone has a dead battery or is otherwise unresponsive when someone else tries the power button. In reality the screen is on, just not displaying anything, and you need to trace a pre-defined unlock gesture or perform some combination of button presses to awaken the beast.

Keeper *des sleutels*

LastPass

If you're wise, you'll have different passwords for all the accounts you have dotted around the Internet. LastPass is a free password manager and generator allowing you to keep all your logins, passwords and PINs in one secure, encrypted database and access it with a single master password. It syncs well with other devices, can autocomplete your passwords and online forms and has a plugin version for most major browsers. Although the desktop version is free to use, the Android app requires a premium subscription at $1 per month. For an alternative, try **mSecure Password Manager**.

KeePassDroid

Similar to LastPass in that it allows you to keep all your logins, passwords and PINs in a secure database (encrypted with AES and Twofish, the most secure encryption algorithms currently known), accessible with one master password. The main difference is that the database is stored locally on your devices (or synced via Dropbox). A little less convenient than LastPass, it feels more secure as a result.

Screen Lock Bypass

Locked out of your phone or tablet and can't recall the passcode? As a last resort you can point your computer's web browser to the Google Play™ website and install this app to your device. As the name suggests it'll bypass the lock screen, allowing you to access your stuff again. The app won't actually fix your forgotten unlock code, but you can use the opportunity to back everything up and start again.

Malware & theft protection

avast! Mobile Security

Free security suite packing a list of features you'd be paying around $20 a year for from other services like **Lookout** and **Mcafee Wavesecure** (though these are also well worth your consideration). You get a virus and malware scanner, a privacy advisor, which examines your installed apps' permissions and alerts you to any potential risks, an application manager, web shield to protect against malicious or phishing sites, a firewall (root users only) to prevent selected apps from connecting to the Internet, an SMS and call filter for blocking specific contacts, and an anti-theft service which lets you lock down your phone if lost or stolen, and send SMS commands to enable GPS tracking, secure erase, siren activation, audio monitoring and more.

Where's My Droid

The original Android™ phone locator and still one of the best. For those where-did-I-put-it moments, it'll make your phone ring out loud so that you can find it down the back of the sofa, in a pizza box, or anywhere else within earshot. Still can't find it? You can track GPS location, lock your device, remotely wipe phone and SD data and more.

Plan B

Last resort tracking app that you can remotely install on a device (using Google Play™ on your desktop web browser) even after it's already been lost. Once installed, it'll send details of your phone's location to your Gmail™ address, and will send an update every time you text the word "locate" to your lost phone.

Privacy

aSpotCat

Your device's application settings page provides an overview of services your apps can access and can give you a general idea about whether there are any potential privacy issues. aSpotCat gives you a greater level of detail, and lists your installed apps by permission, so you can see, for example, all the apps that access your GPS location or use services

like SMS that can cost you money. For more permission snooping, try **Permission Dog** or **Suspicious Apps**. Root users can also try **Permissions Denied**, which will let you switch off specific permissions for any apps you want to restrict.

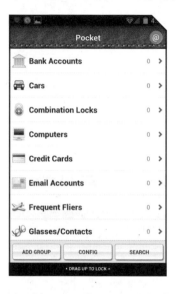

 Pocket

If you want to keep sensitive data, like your bank account details or passwords, handy on your mobile device but are worried about them getting into the wrong hands, try Pocket. It lets you securely store any information you like in one place, securely encrypted. Items are stored in a range of categories (bank accounts, credit cards, passports, serial numbers and so on) with the capacity to add more of your own. It also, rather sensibly, self-locks after a set timeout and routinely clears the clipboard of any copy-and-pasted passwords or other information.

 App Lock

Got certain apps you'd like to envelop in an extra layer of security? You can use this app (and many others of a similar nature) to protect selected applications (including built-in ones like SMS, Camera, USB connection and so on) with a passcode (numeric or pattern). It's easy to configure, presenting you with a list of your apps and system settings. Just set the toggle switch to lock your preferred items.

Backup

MyBackup Pro

The most comprehensive non-root backup solution (root users, look no further than **Titanium Backup Pro**). MyBackup allows for heaps of data, including SMS, MMS, call logs, contacts, bookmarks, your custom dictionary, playlists, system settings, apps, alarms and more to be backed up to your SD card or on the developer RerWare's own servers. Backups can be triggered manually or scheduled to run automatically and the items to back up are selectable from a check list. Useful if you're switching phones and want to move stuff across, or if you intend to factory reset your device and want a quick way to restore your settings.

Ultimate Backup Pro

An excellent solution for backing up and managing apps, including batch and automated backups, a task manager and an apps-to-SD manager. Root users can also take advantage of app data backup, automated uninstalls, permission disabling and a whole host of other advanced features.

Shopping
Til you drop

We all do it; it's nothing to be ashamed of. Whether you're looking for a bargain or just looking for the way out of the supermarket, there are plenty of apps out there to help you empty your pockets along the way.

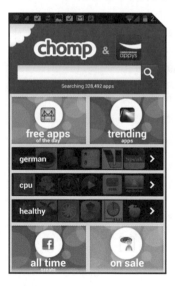

Chomp

Ever tried searching Google Play™ and come away feeling like there's something you missed? Chomp is an app for app shopping: a search engine that searches apps by function and topic, allowing you to find an app based on what it does, rather than what it's called. As if this wasn't useful enough, you can filter results, browse all the paid apps currently on special offer and more. We wish we'd found this one before writing this book, it would have been so much easier.

Mighty Grocery Shopping List

Powerful shopping list manager supporting multiple lists, cost calculation including taxes, coupons and more. You can select from a pre-set list of items, sort them by aisle and check them off as you work your way around the store. You can also speak a list of items you'd like to add, along with quantities, weights and prices and have all of these added to your list.

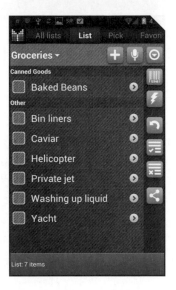

The full version also features a barcode scanner, list sync, recipes and a broader range of configuration options. American readers can also try **Grocery IQ**.

Our Groceries

No more running back out to the corner store. This little shopping app lets multiple users sync to the same live grocery list, allowing items to be amended remotely. It's also available in iPhone, BlackBerry and web versions, so everyone can stay synced no matter what device they're using. See items being checked off as your partner progresses around the supermarket, add last-minute items, or separate off and grab different products without picking up duplicates.

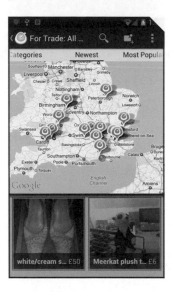

EggDrop – Local Marketplace

Free classified ads in the US and UK. Browse items locally or list your own with a few quick snaps from your device's camera. You can also list wanted items and set your preferred price, plus share your ads directly with Facebook, Twitter and Craigslist. The app lets you chat with sellers in real time and leave feedback for your transactions. There are no listing fees, the only real downside for UK users is the current lack of people using the app, but hopefully this will pick up over time. US users are spoilt for choice when it comes to mobile classifieds: check out **CraigsList Browser** or **Milo Local Shopping**.

Key Ring Reward Cards

Lets you scan and store all your reward and loyalty cards on your phone, sign up for new reward schemes and get discount coupons from participating retailers. You may have mixed results getting the on-screen barcode display to scan properly at the checkout, so don't throw all your cards away just yet. For an alternative, try **FidMe – Loyalty cards** or **CardStar**.

Google Shopper

Kind of a reworking of other Google™ products in the name of buying stuff, Shopper™ lets you snap product barcodes and cover artwork for instant online price comparisons and reviews. It also hits you with local deals and special offers. It's also worth trying **Red Laser**.

Pocket Auctions for eBay

No-fuss access to your eBay account, including live countdowns, a barcode scanner and a price check function that lets you view searched items finishing within your price range, as well as comparing prices with similar items outside of eBay. It also sends notifications when your watched items are about to end. A great, lightweight way to keep your eye on the ball with your eBay bids. If you want to sell stuff from your Android™ device you'll need the **Official eBay Android App**, which lets you enter listings quickly with the help of a barcode scanner.

Discount Calculator

Some apps try to throw as many features at you as they can, while others just do one thing but do it well. This app lets you quickly calculate store discount or sale prices based on percentage, and can factor sales tax into your final price.

MySizeFinder

Helps you find the right women's clothes sizes for different brands, useful if buying online or shopping for a gift when the item can't be tried on for size. For size conversions between countries, try **Simple Clothes Converter**.

Social
Friends and followers

Whichever social networks you use on a regular basis, you'll find an official app on Google Play™, along with a plethora of unofficial alternatives. Generally the official apps are a pretty good starting point, with their counterparts often offering one or two overlooked features.

Plume

Nicely designed and customizable Twitter client, supporting multiple accounts, geotagging, URL shortening and Twitpic photo upload. It auto-completes hash tags and user names, and lets you colourize or mute individual tweeters. Drag the bar at the top for a pull-down area for writing your own tweets. Conversations, profiles and replies are all displayed inline, and it has some beautiful widgets (as you'd expect from the makers of **Beautiful Widgets**). Other fine Twitter clients include **Tweetcaster** and **Twicca**.

Facebook

At present the official Facebook app appears to have settled into a form that's largely indistinguishable from the mobile site, which is actually quite a good thing, considering some of its earlier incarnations. Most of the site's features are present, including chat, within a side panel that hides away when not needed. It seems to have caught up with the apps that stepped in to fill the void when earlier releases fell short of the mark. The main fault with the app is that it no longer syncs contacts with Android™ 2.3 or later, but this can be remedied by installing **Facebook contact Sync** or **HaxSync**.

Friendcaster

Friendcaster always managed to squeeze in most of the functionality that was until recently absent from the official Facebook app. It's still worth a look though, for its reliable notification support with a quick-reply facility, pull-to-refresh status updates, add/remove and favourite lists for friends, in-app photo editing and tagging, easy link sharing from the browser, events and groups, built-in chat, and some pleasant-looking widgets for grabbing a quick update from your home screen. It lets you select privacy settings for individual posts and supports SSL encryption for added security. It also manages to sync contacts without the need for a third-party application.

Google+

Google™'s social network combines elements of Facebook and Twitter while adding a few tricks of its own. The Stream section gives you a standard issue timeline of the people you're following, allowing you to "+1" an entry (Google's equivalent of a "like"), add comments, re-share and so on. Other sections let you view and tag photos, manage your circles (separate clumps of friends and aquaintances) and the people in them, and group chat. It syncs contacts seamlessly with your main contact list (you can choose which circles to sync) and has a convenient instant upload option, which sends any photos you take directly to your account.

Seesmic

A decent, simple aggregator that pulls in content from your Twitter, Facebook and Salesforce Chatter accounts. Facebook integration lets you read and post status updates, comments and likes, and manage any pages you administer, but stops short of providing chat, photo albums or many of the other features offered by a dedicated client. The Twitter side of things is better equipped, supporting multiple accounts, cross-posting, lists, retweets, conversations and more.

HootSuite

Aimed at PR professionals, HootSuite combines Twitter, Facebook, Google+, Foursquare and LinkedIn streams into a single screen for each identity you have, keeping track of mentions, messages, retweets and so on. You can post updates to all your networks at once or pick individual ones, and syndicate RSS feeds from your blogs or anywhere else into your accounts. Basic accounts are free, and include enough functionality for most non-corporate users. HootSuite has the edge over other aggregators in that it also provides a web client, meaning you can log in from your desktop and still get all your networks in one place through a familiar interface.

Foursquare

Location-based social network focused very much on going out rather than staying in. Foursquare lets you "check in" to bars, venues and other meeting places. You can pick up tips about the best places to go, find out where your friends are, and get freebies and discounts from participating businesses.

Thumb

Ask a question and get answers and opinions, either from your friends or the general public. Users give you a thumbs up or thumbs down, and can add comments to support their vote. Results start to come in surprisingly quickly, indicating that there are a lot of people out there with way too much time on their hands. For more involved questions and answers, check **Formspring**.

Glympse

Lets you send your current location or a shared destination to friends via email, SMS, Facebook or Twitter. Locations can expire after a set duration or ended manually. At the receiving end, your friend gets a web link to a Google Map™ with your whereabouts on it. If you move, the map updates accordingly, until the location expires. There's no need to sign up for anything, or for your recipient to install anything at their end, which makes a refreshing change.

Badoo – Meet New People

New in town, or just sick of the same old faces? This app helps you meet new people in your area, chat, date or just hang out. For more slightly ambiguous is-it-a-dating-site-or-not fun, try **Tagged**. Or for not-so-ambiguous dating, try **OKCupid Dating**.

Posterous Spaces

Set up ad hoc spaces for sharing photos, videos and text content publicly, or between a private group of contributing friends. Spaces can then be shared with your social networks and other locations around the web.

Sports
A load of balls

Some sports are better represented than others in the Android™ realm. Soccer, golf and cycling seem to account for a large portion of the apps on offer, with the remainder taken up with hunting calls and fishing advice. If you're looking to follow a particular team or get live scores for a certain sport, you're probably in luck. Here's a selection of the most interesting sport-related apps we could dig up.

LiveScore
Get real-time results from around the world directly to your Android. Covers football/soccer, tennis, basketball and ice hockey. For more scores coverage, try **ScoreMobile for Android**. For dedicated soccer scores, try **Soccer Livescores** or **Goal.com Mobile**. For Cricket, check out **Crickbuzz**.

ESPN ScoreCenter
More global live scores, news in-game stats, game summaries and league tables for everything from Formula One racing to tennis to basketball. Follow your favourite teams or get updates on the most important live events of the day, with video clips, editorial analysis and more.

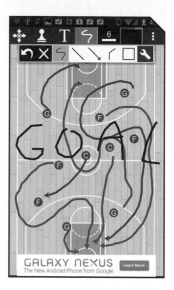

Basketball Dood

One of a series of playbook apps for different team sports (other apps available include **Hockey Dood**, **Soccer Dood**, **Baseball Dood** and more). You can create animated play drills, move players around and add doodles and text.

Fantasy Football Manager

Everything you could need to manage your fantasy team, drag and drop players into position, see injured players, view fixtures, match results, and sort teams and players with a useful range of filters. For more, try **Fantasy Football Buddy**. For other sports, try Yahoo! Inc's offerings.

Strava Cycling

Track your cycling distances and times over GPS and compare results with friends and locals. The app stores maps of your rides and gives you detailed statistics, including pace, elevation, calories and more. You can also earn achievements, such as becoming the King or Queen of specific roads or trails. And you thought you were just getting to work and back on the cheap.

FixtureBox

Never miss a game again. This sports calendar covers over two hundred major leagues and competitions worldwide. When your teams or players have a match, the fixtures are added to your calendar, along with home and away teams, venue locations and start times, and will update automatically if times or dates are changed. From football, soccer and rugby to tennis, cycling or boxing, most major sports are covered. For catching live matches on TV, try **Thuuz**.

Bike Repair

This step-by-step bicycle repair and maintenance guide covers more than seventy different problems and how to fix them, in an easily navigable interface. Bike Repair is quite a large app, roling in at 46MB. For a lightweight alternative (at under 3MB), try **Bike Doctor**.

SkyDroid – Golf GPS

Don't let the shonky logo put you off, this GPS-based golf range-finder shows your distance from the green, or to any point on the course. It includes satellite maps of over 22,000 golf courses (full list available at skydroid.net), complete with hazards, bunkers and more. Need even more golf GPS in your life? Check out **FreeCaddie Pro Golf GPS**. For keeping score, take a look at **Easy Scorecard**.

Ski & Snow Report

One to check before you hit the slopes. Offers ski reports, a five-day weather forecast, live cams and first-hand reports from other skiers.

Cue Tool

Swiss Army knife for pool players (and you never even knew you needed one!). Includes a coin toss, scoreboard with timer, tips, tricks and lessons and more.

Sports Timer Pro

Stopwatch with lap, parallel and multiple time modes. Ideal for keeping track times for yourself or multiple participants at the same time.

Skullcandy

All-in-one tool for board sports – surfing, skating and snowboarding, with streaming music (presumably the kinds of genres people into these sports are meant to like by default; hip-hop, thrash, contemporary avant-garde and so on).

Each zone (surf, snow, etc) has global weather and conditions reports, favourite destinations with five-day forecasts, GPS search for rad slopes, sick waves or the nearest bitchin skate park (not usually within walking distance from one another). There's also plenty of related video content. Sadly it doesn't currently have a user-submitted poetry section, but otherwise it, like, totally shreds.

Tools
Utilities, reference and more

The Tools section is probably one of the most useful areas of Google Play™. It's full of unassuming little utilities that often end up being the most used applications on your device.

Utilities

Tiny Flashlight + LED

One of many all-singing, all-dancing flashlight apps, using your device's camera LED flash as a surprisingly bright torch. This one also provides strobe effects and various screen lights, including amber warning lights, flashing police lights and a text to Morse Code generator. For a no-fuss on/off LED widget, try **LED Light**.

Boxmeup

Moving house? Burying pieces of your latest victim all over town? You can use this app to make an inventory of what you've put into each box, and then generate a QR code label to stick on the box. At the other end, scan the codes to reveal the contents of each box.

Wi-Fi Analyzer

Dodgy connection? Get a quick window on who's battling you for the airwaves. Wi-Fi Analyzer shows all the nearby Wi-Fi access points and helps you improve your own Wi-Fi signal at home by finding a less crowded channel for your wireless router. It offers a number of different views of the state of your airwaves, including a channel graph and a signal strength meter. With the free add-on Wi-Fi Connector, it even lets you switch connections from within the app.

LED Scroller

Type in your phrase, select your LED on/off colours and scrolling speed and this little app will turn your Android™ into a delightful scrolling LED display.

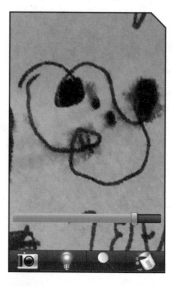

Ultra Magnifier +

Magnifying apps usually don't offer much more than your device's camera and zoom can. This one provides a little extra, with clear, crisp images and a much steadier and more consistent auto-focus. It also offers colour effect options (negative, mono and so on), an in-app camera and LED torch. Handy for reading the small print on your phone contract.

Prox

Uses the proximity sensor and accelerometer to give you gesture-based control over your phone without the need to even touch it. Magically waft your hand about like some kind of wizard to launch apps, expand the notification bar and silence your phone (you can say "Be Silent!" with a faraway look in your eye for effect if you like, but this is optional). Useful app for masters of illusion and people with no fingers.

AppGarden

Dozens of micro utilities in one tiny app, AppGarden comprises a useful collection of calculators, lookup tools, converters and more. Everything from airport codes, dictionary, and body mass index to an album art finder, mortgage calculator, stopwatch, URL shortener and many more.

AppZilla

Another all-in-one utility selection. It's easy on the eye, but like a lot of these multi-tools, it tends to be a jack of all trades, master of none; but it does offer the convenience of having everything you could need in one app. For more of this kind of thing, try **Super Swiss Army Knife** or **Smart Tools**.

CloudMagic

A lookup tool that can perform lightning-fast searches across your online accounts, including Exchange, Twitter, Gmail™, Docs, Chat, Calendar and Contacts. Check it out if you don't mind the potential security implications of handing access to these services over to a third-party app.

Onavo Data Usage Monitor

Monitors your mobile data usage (4G, 3G and so on), lets you know when you're getting close to your monthly limit, and helps you identify which apps are hogging your bandwidth. If you're not on an ulimited data plan, you probably need this app. Alternately, try **3G Watchdog**.

Barcode Scanner

Scans barcodes, data matrix and QR codes, and lets you look up prices, URLs, app installations and more.

Bubble

Turns your device into a spirit-level, either on its side, or flat on its back for a 360° level. It can also display the angle as a number, speak it out loud, and beep when completely level.

Advanced Ruler Pro

Works as both an accurate on-screen ruler and camera-based height and distance calculator. The latter takes a little diligence to ensure an accurate reading, but if you need one, this is the tool for the job.

tTorrent

Downloading torrents to an Android device seems like a pretty good way to eat up all your SD memory, but if you need one, tTorrent is one of the best torrent clients available for the platform (in lieu of the official µTorrent client, rumoured to be coming soon), sporting most of the features offered by fully grown desktop clients. Alternatively, try **TorrentFu**, or if you want to manage your desktop µTorrent progress remotely, try **µTorrent Remote** (p.116).

Reference

ElectroDroid

Must-have tool for anyone messing with electronics, this little app has everything from a resistor colour code identifier to pinout diagrams for dozens of connector types, reference tables, calculators and much more. To set up and test circuits in a virtual environment, try **EveryCircuit**.

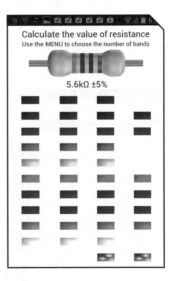

ConvertPad – Unit Converter

Convert virtually anything that's convertible. For a comparably capable converter with a slightly friendlier interface, try **gUnit – Unit Converter**.

File managers

ES File Explorer

Everything you could possibly need in a file manager, ES File Explorer not only lets you explore and edit the files stored on your Android™ device, but can also connect via Wi-Fi and Bluetooth to provide access to files on your home computer and other devices, local area network and the Internet. It has a built-in FTP client and cloud storage client with support for Dropbox, SugarSync and Box.com. As if all this wasn't enough, it also includes file viewers, a text editor, compressed and encrypted file support, an application manager and task killer. Other exceptional file managers worth a look are **File Expert** and **Astro File Manager**.

X-Plore File Manager

Desktop-style dual-pane file manager with expandable folder trees. Includes most of the extraneous features of other modern file managers, but in a more familiar, easily navigable interface.

Wi-Fi file explorer Pro

Simple to use, feature-rich app which opens

up your device's Wi-Fi file management possibilities. No more messing around with USB cables; you can browse, transfer, edit and even stream files to and from your Android device via a web browser and Wi-Fi connection.

AirDroid

Control your Android device from your computer's web browser. More than just a file transfer app, AirDroid gives you complete file management, along with the ability to read and send SMS messages, install and uninstall apps, view photos, edit contacts and ringtones and more.

Bluetooth file transfer

Handy little app that lets you securely browse, explore, share and manage files and contacts on nearby Bluetooth devices. It has a fast, customizable file browser and can even search within and create compressed (Zip, Tar and GZip) archives.

The File Converter

Converts between a useful range of file formats, covering popular audio, video, eBook, document, image and archive file types. Need to convert FLAC into MP3, or 3GP into MKV? Look no further.

System tools

SystemPanel

Combines a task manager, app manager and system monitor. It gives you a clear live view of which apps are using your device's processor and memory, and monitors them over time to provide a detailed history of their activities. It'll also let you back up multiple versions of apps (useful to fall back on if an app you were using suddenly updates itself to a version that doesn't work any more). For alternatives, try **Android Assistant** or **System Tuner Pro**. If all you need is a basic task killer, try **Advanced Task Killer**.

Apps 2 SD

It can be a drag manually checking every single installed app to see if moving it to SD memory is possible. Apps 2 SD rounds up all your moveable apps in one place and lets you decide which ones to move. It also gives you a one-click option to migrate them all at the same time.

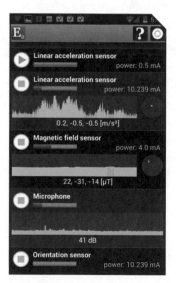

Elixir II

System information with a great selection of widgets, covering just about every aspect of your device from CPU usage to sensor readings (accelerometer, proximity sensor, etc). Change settings, perform SD and cache operations, and toggle everything from USB tethering to screen rotation.

DiskUsage

Gives you a complete visual overview of your device's storage. Zoom in and out and tap items to view them. An invaluable tool for hunting down space-hogging apps and files.

Smart Rotator

Lets you control which apps are able to auto-rotate on screen and specify whether they should default to portrait or landscape.

Andmade Share

Enhances your system's share facility, allowing you to re-shuffle the destination list and send stuff to multiple applications at once.

Juice Defender

Squeeze every last bit of juice out of your battery with this automated power manager. It lets you tinker to your heart's content, specifying precise criteria for (among other things) the behaviour of your device's power-hungry Wi-Fi and mobile data functions, based on such things as time of day, location or current battery level. For example, you can

set Wi-Fi so that it's only enabled when the screen is on, but schedule it to open up for a minute every so often to allow synchronization. The included widgets let you easily switch key functions on or off and tell you how much juice you've saved. For a simple alternative, try **Easy Battery Saver**.

App Cache Cleaner

Free up internal memory on your device by clearing your apps' stored cache and data files. One tap cleans out the lot, or you can select individual apps to target.

Fing – Network Tools

Full network management toolkit, including network discovery, service scan, ping, traceroute, DNS lookup, TCP connection tester and more.

ZDBox (All-In-One toolbox)

An excellent collection of system-oriented utilities and widgets, giving you better control over your device, with sound settings, screen rotation, Wi-Fi, GPS, one-tap battery saving mode, data usage monitor, app lock, cache cleaner and more.

Transportation
Going places

Your Android™ device's GPS antenna and compass make it an ideal tool for finding your way around. In addition to the apps mentioned here, it's worth noting that public transport timetables and maps are available as apps for most major cities around the globe, so check before travelling to see if any good options exist for your specific destination.

Planes

FlightTrack

Gives you real-time flight tracking, with departure and arrival information, zoomable live tracking maps with weather imagery, info on delays (with detailed forecasts and updates sent to your notification bar), gate numbers, cancellations and help finding an alternative flight. You can share your flight status via SMS, email, Twitter or any other messaging app. It'll even check your seat number against SeatGuru's plane seating maps. Whether travelling yourself or picking someone up from the airport, this will keep you up to date on a flight's progress (or lack of it). For a free alternative, try **FlightView**.

OnTheFly

Great tool for quickly searching cheap flights across multiple airlines. For more, try **KAYAK** (p.162), or **SkyScanner**.

Gate Guru

Nice little resource for your day of travel, with updated airport security waiting times, airport food, shops and facilities, reviews and more. It also integrates with your KAYAK and TripIt (p.162) itineraries.

Trains, buses & taxis

Öffi – Public Transport

Impressive public transport timetables, with live arrival and departure details covering most of the UK and Europe, as well as some locations in Australia and the US. When viewing a list of local departure points, each has a live compass showing its direction, great for finding a bus stop or station in a strange city. It also features a downloadable library of transport network maps from around the world. For more world transport and subway network maps, try **aMetro – World Subway Maps**.

cab4me

Hooks you up swiftly with local cab companies, along with user ratings, contacts access for pickup location search, and GPS map displaying taxi ranks in relation to your current location. Londoners, try **Hailo Black Cab & Taxi**. US users can try **Taxi Magic**.

Navigation

Waze

Increasingly popular social driving and navigation app, using community-contributed updates on congestion, road hazards, speed traps and more. It incorporates this information into its turn-by-turn navigation, giving you estimated journey times based on the current traffic situation and re-routing your journey to avoid problem areas. Contributing updates of your own is easy, with a grid of icons you can quickly tap to add relevant updates to your current location.

Google Maps

An unparalleled resource for anyone who ever leaves their home. As well as mapping, excellent turn-based navigation for drivers, walkers and public transport users with live traffic updates, you get local business search and reviews, interactive street-view and internal maps of airports, shopping malls, stadiums and other large public structures.

Sygic

Google Maps™ and Navigation are great but they do rely on an Internet or data connection in order to function properly. Sygic offers full offline turn-by-turn voice-guided navigation, transforming your Android™ device into a fully equipped sat-nav using the latest TomTom maps. The display is exceptional, with amazing 3D rendering of cities and landscape. Maps are available to buy in a range of country or continent packs.

CoPilot Live

Another fully operational voice-guided offline sat-nav. Features include detailed 2D and 3D maps, speed camera alerts, and live traffic and fuel price updates. As with Sygic, packages are available for different world zones.

Trapster

Similar to Waze, this app focuses more specifically on speed cameras and police cars on the road. Invaluable tool for plotting the getaway for your next bank job. For more, try **EZCam Speed Camera Detector**.

OsmAnd

Open-source alternative to Google Maps, with Wikipedia links to places of interest and offline search, and pedestrian, bicycle and car-mode navigation.

Cars

Torque/Torque Pro

If your car has OBD (on-board diagnostics), Torque will connect to it via Bluetooth and glean all sorts of valuable diagnostic information about performance, faults and sensor readings. Set up a dashboard with widgets and gauges and see what your car is doing in real time.

WhatGas Petrol Prices Pro

Live, community-updated petrol prices in your current vicinity, shown on a map. Presently it has a small user base, so prices aren't always as up to date as they could be, but as this increases it could become as useful as **GasBuddy**, an excellent app currently only serving US and Canadian drivers.

Car Home Ultra

Lets you easily and safely access your phone while driving. It provides a speedometer, compass, clock, weather report, media player controls and customizable shortcuts to other apps and functions, all within a large icon-based interface. It can also automatically transfer all your calls to speakerphone. For an alternative, try **Car Dashboard Pro**.

My Car Locator

Saves your parking position and helps you navigate back there later, with map views and an arrow that indicates the direction of your vehicle. Other fine car-finding apps include **Car Finder AR**.

Travel and local
Out and about

From maps and location-aware content, transport and hotel booking to geocaching your movements around the globe, these apps make your Android™ device an easy travel companion.

Travel tools

WiFi Finder
Connect to free and paid Wi-Fi hotspots around the globe. Results are shown on a map and a 360° proximity graph. ICS users, try **Free Zone Wi-Fi**.

QuickDic
Indispensable translation dictionary, QuickDic is fast, ad-free and stores dictionaries on your device's

SD card for offline translation. Converts English to fifty or so other languages. For more functions, try **Google Translate** (p.44).

PolyClock World Clock

World clock with an exquisite variety of widgets, showing daylight and darkness hours, map view and globe view with time zones. For even more eye candy, try **TerraTime**, or for less, try the free **World Clock & Widget**.

XE Currency

Converts all world currencies, with live updates, historical charts and more. If you find this app to be slight overkill for travelling and want a more lightweight solution, try **Currency Converter** by Oanda.

Emergency Live Tracker

Sends email and SMS alerts showing your location to your pre-selected contacts in an emergency situation, say if you broke your ankle hiking, or crashed your car in a remote ditch or got kidnapped or caught in an earthquake, or chewed on by bears.

Mosquito Repellent

Generates high frequency sounds that mosquitoes simply cannot deal with. Alternatively, you can generate your own using **Favorite Frequencies**.

Local info

Aloqa – Always Be A Local

Interesting take on the whole "what's nearby" service, Aloqa lets you subscribe to "channels": basically feeds from existing services such as LastFM, Yelp, OpenTable and others, to find events, gigs, galleries, restaurants and more based on your current location. The app allows for favouriting venues and events, setting up a profile based on your interests and checking in with Facebook, and can also push new items to your notification bar. For more, try **Poynt** or **Yelp**. US readers can also try **Where**.

Google Places

Fire up Places™ from a selected Google Maps™ location for all kinds of local information: restaurants, cafés, pubs, entertainment, ATMs, hotels, taxis and more. Select a category and peruse the reviews (or add your own), get directions, see photos, or call them. It also links to other social reviewing networks (Qype, beerintheevening and plenty of others) for a broader overview of the establishment in question.

Qype

Social networking meets social reviewing. You can set up a profile and make friends if you want to, or just ignore that side of it and use the invaluable real-life reviews from real-life customers. Find Places gives you a more navigable paring-down of your options than Google Places™, based on what you're actually looking for. It also offers discount vouchers for participating local businesses.

Wikitude World Browser

Point your Android™ device's camera at the world around you for an augmented reality overlay with tags for places of interest, restaurants, bars, ATMs and so on. Tap a tag for more information, including content from Wikipedia, YouTube™ and Twitter. For more augmented reality, try **Layar**.

TripAdvisor

Lets you browse thousands of user reviews of restaurants, bars and hotel rooms, making for an excellent travel companion. You can also contribute reviews of your own.

HearPlanet: World Audio Guide

Talking tour guide covering three hundred thousand locations worldwide. A map lets you quickly discover featured places in your vicinity, or you can browse the planet, listening to guides for anything that takes your interest.

Buildings

Mobile encyclopedia of more than forty thousand awesome buildings worldwide, with photos, historical information, user comments and more. Find interesting architecture nearby on (you guessed it) a Google Map, or simply browse the buildings of the world at your leisure.

National Trust

Remember playing hide-and-seek in a derelict castle or cavorting up and down long wood-panelled rooms screaming while your parents ambled around trying to sustain interest in a seemingly endless supply of suits of arms, stuffed animal heads, and glass cases full of yellowed books, old horse brushes and embossed handkerchiefs? For anyone travelling around the UK, or just looking for a nice day out, the official National Trust app is a great starting point. All the sites are map located, and there's plenty of visitor information and photos to help you make your choice.

Travel booking

TripIt

An indispensable travel organizer. Forward booking confirmations (from flights, hotels, restaurants and more) to the supplied email address and the details will appear in your TripIt itinerary and also sync with your calendar. Wave goodbye to carrying a sheaf of dog-eared printouts around with you every time you travel. For an alternative, try **WorldMate**.

KAYAK

Lets you compare prices for flights, hotels and car hire, track flight status, manage your itinerary and check baggage fees. For a similar service, try **Hipmunk**.

booking.com

Fantastic browser for finding and booking hotel rooms. For more, try **Hotels.com**. Bargain hunters, try **priceline Hotel Negotiator**. Rolled into town late? For last-minute bargains, try **Hotel Tonight**.

Caravan Buddy

Search, book and navigate to camping and caravan sites around the UK. For the rest of Europe, try **Alan Rogers Camping** or **iCampsites**.

Travel journals & geocaching

Trip Journal

Tracks and maps your location while you upload photos, video and journal entries, and makes it all instantly available through your social network of choice. It integrates well with YouTube™, Picasa™, Flickr, Twitter, Facebook and Google Earth™ and lets friends make envious comments on your progress. Well thought out and easy to use, media-rich travelogue. For a free alternative, try **OnTheRoad**.

Locus Pro

Hiking navigation and geocaching app supporting both online and offline maps from a range of sources and formats. The app also provides weather and parking information, notification of nearby points of interest, and supports add-ons, allowing integration with Google My Maps™, Street View™, Breadcrumbs, Foursquare and other services. For more, try **BackCountry Navigator** or **Maverick Pro**.

Weather

or not it's raining

The weather widgets that ship with your device usually provide perfectly adequate weather forecasting. Collections such as Beautiful Widgets (p.102) also offer some exceptional animated weather information. But if you can't help feeling you need a little something extra, read on.

Weatherwise
Delightfully atmospheric app which displays the weather as an animated illustration. Comes with a free tree theme (shown here), with more themes available to purchase in-app, including The Woobles (creepy one-eyed monsters), 8 bit (a pixel art windmill) and Lost Robot (a giant half-dead robot tangled up in weird forestry).

1Weather
A weather app that actually manages to not look like a confusing mess. 1Weather gives you simple, no-fuss icons for live weather and multi-day forecasts.

WeatherBug
Never stick your hand out the window ever again: this app covers UV data, pollen count, temperature, lightning strikes, humidity, air pressure, wind speed, cloud cover. The ad-free "Elite" version offers live wallpapers, additional map layers, forecast and map widgets and live radar animation. For hour-by-hour forecasts in less detail, try **The Weather Channel**.

Piri Pollen
If you don't mind the Piriton branding, this is a great app for pollen count forecasts in your area, showing data for different pollen types (trees, grasses, etc).

Radioactivity Counter
Transforms your Android™ device's camera into a working radioactivity meter. You'll need to cover the lens with some black tape first though. Unfortunately we recently had all of our weapons-grade plutonium confiscated so are unable to test its effectiveness.

Earthquake Alert!
Some gifted individuals are able to notice the subtle cues that indicate there's an earthquake going on right under their feet. For the rest of us, there's this. It also alerts you to any earthquakes going on in the rest of the world, in case that proves useful.

Weird

The strangest apps in town

In the course of writing this book, we stumbled across some pretty bizarre apps. Here's a selection of some of the weirdest.

In-Gut MAZE

Guide the little flying saucer through a maze of cute intestines and gasp in awe as it arrives in a toilet bowl as a variety of different anthropomorphized poop formations.

I'm Rich!! (White Diamond)

The ultimate status symbol. This £80 app simply displays a diamond icon on your home screen with the words "I'm Rich". More fun for the 1% can be found with **High Rollers Club Black Diamond**.

My Boyfriend Generator

Generates fake boyfriend identities so that you can more effectively lie about being in a relationship when you're not. Also comes in a girlfriend variety.

Wet Cement

Having trouble finding recently poured wet cement to write your name on? You're in luck! Use this app to get notifications of wet cement near you, geotag wet cement of your own or upload photos of wet cement.

PoopLog

Keep a detailed daily record of your bowel movements, attach photos and share with your Facebook and Twitter followers. Great if you're having trouble generating logs of your own. If you need a little help, try **Bio Feedback Constipation Clinic**.

I Eat Cockroaches

Lets you fill a virtual drinking glass with cockroaches and then chug it down. There's also a Pro version which includes larvae.

Magic Hands

"Use this app to take pictures of where you want David the Healer to put his Magic Hands! Give it a try and see if you can feel the Magic Hands touching you. Many have written back confirming they felt the hands."

Easy Shredding

Tap the screen to shred the cabbage. Why would you not want an app that could do this?

Milk The Cow
Udderly amazing app that lets you practice milking a cow. Handy for when civilization breaks down and you really want a cup of tea but can't buy milk in the shops.

Awkward Turtle
Ever found yourself struggling to keep a conversation going. This app suggests random facts to help you change the subject. Phrases like "A donkey will sink in quicksand but a mule won't" should enable you to create a distraction long enough to slip out the back door.

Fingers Versus Knife
Stab the knife down between your fingers as fast as you can. Oops, there goes another one! For more harmful fun, try **Ultimate Russian Roulette**.

PooPee Animals! For Kids
Tap on any of the strange, bobble-headed farmyard animals wandering around on the screen and they emit a fart. All of the animals then turn to face you and laugh menacingly. Keep playing to unlock zebras, elephants and other mammals.

games

Games

Just press play

Developers have moved quickly to show what's possible with the Android™ platform, and the ever-expanding gaming section on Google Play™ is helpfully browsable by category (Arcade & Action, Brain & Puzzle and more).

Kongregate Arcade

Flash-based gaming site Kongregate has an Android app that gives you access to their mountain of free games – over six hundred at the time of writing – more than enough to keep you busy. Create an account and you can compete with friends on leader boards, rate and review games, collect badges and track your scores.

OnLive

Buy or rent console and PC games then stream them to your phone or tablet (or your Mac/PC/ games console). Games are cross-platform, allowing you to pick up a game in the evening on your console that you started on the train to work using your phone. You can play using on-screen touch controls, or buy OnLive's wireless controller from onlive.com/store.

Brain & puzzle

 ### Drop7

Whatever it was you were planning on getting done today, forget it. This compelling Tetris-like number game gets more addictive the more you play it. Rack up the numbers and they explode in time with the hypnotic Philip Glass-esque soundtrack, uncovering more numbers as they go.

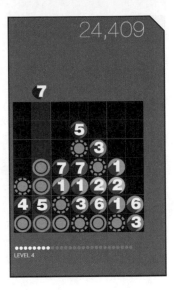

Lettered

Tilt or rotate your screen and the letters slide around. Freeze letters in place and move the other letters around them to make words. Can you clear enough words before the screen fills up? It also has a Boggle-like mode where you have to find as many words as you can from a random grid. A nice touch with both modes is that you can set the size of the grid.

 ### Slice It!

Presents you with a series of shapes to cut into equally sized pieces. It starts you out with a couple of no-brainers but before you know it, things start to get tricky.

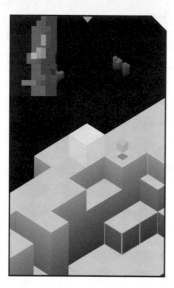

 ## Edge

Sublimely beautiful block game wherein you guide a dazzling, colour-shifting cube around a clean white maze of walkways, towers, switches and moving obstacles. An engaging, visual treat.

 ## Burn The Rope

Set the rope burning and rotate the screen to keep the flame alive. Things get pretty complicated once you start having to burn different coloured bugs in order to burn through different colours of rope, but you don't have to be an expert in string theory to get the most out of this game.

 ## Apparatus

Beautifully rendered construction puzzle where the objective is to coax the little blue ball into the little blue box, assisted by an array of cables, cogs, generators, ropes, buttons, ball-bearings and other items. As with most Android™ games, it starts you off gently with a couple of easy levels and then hits you with a difficulty curve that takes you from beard-stroking through to head-scratching and ultimately sleep-depriving complexity.

Draw Something

Compete online with friends or random strangers, illustrating the supplied words and guessing your opponents' illustrations, often with hilarious results. Draw Something is extremely popular, with a large user-base, but we found the gameplay a little pedestrian. For a much more fast-paced real-time game against multiple opponents, try **What The Doodle!?**.

Refraction

Use prisms and mirrors to deflect, combine and split coloured beams of light towards their respective targets. It only takes a handful of levels before things start to get fiendishly brain-teasing. For more reflective puzzles, try **Reflexions**.

X Construction

Build a bridge across the ravine, making it sturdy enough for a passenger train to safely rumble across. If your engineering skills aren't up to scratch, well, have you ever seen the movie *The Cassandra Crossing*? It's like that.

Adventure & strategy

Minecraft – Pocket edition

Can you dig it? Minecraft drops you into a strangely beautiful, blocky three-dimensional world populated by pigs, sheep, zombies and other creatures to eat or be eaten by. There's no real objective or direction in the game; you just sort of wander around, collect stuff, make stuff (construct anything from huge cities to complex mechanical traps) and dig yourself deeper and deeper into the ground. Quite a few features of the desktop version are still missing, but these are gradually being added with each update.

Osmos HD

Propel the cell-like being around, engulfing smaller cells and avoiding larger ones (lest they engulf you). By moving, you lose mass, so you'll have to plan your activity carefully. Absorbing stuff!

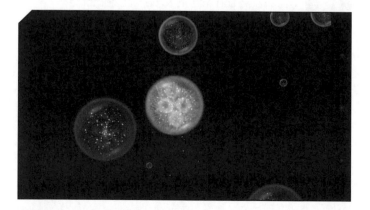

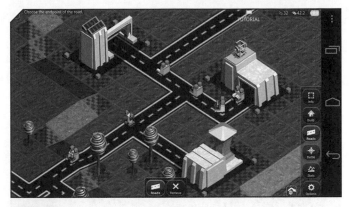

Robotic Planet

Deeply playable strategy game. Build mining stations and factories, and send your robots on attack missions to conquer enemy bases.

Robo Defense

A classic tower defence game and still one of the best. Gun down the bad guys as they try to run into your base. You place gun turrets, flame throwers and magical slow-you-down lava lamps at strategic points outside and hope you have enough firepower to keep them at bay. Killing the bad guys earns you money, which you can spend on bigger guns to kill yet more bigger and badder bad guys. Need more? Try **Fieldrunners HD**.

Great Little War Game

Mobilize your troops through a series of increasingly complicated battlefields in this turn-based strategy game. The game plays like action chess, and you'll have to think ahead if you want to use the varied terrain to your advantage, setting up ambushes and tactically exploiting your enemy's weaknesses.

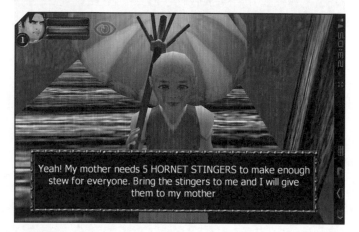

Yeah! My mother needs 5 HORNET STINGERS to make enough stew for everyone. Bring the stingers to me and I will give them to my mother

Earth and Legend

Impressive 3D RPG adventure. It's all villagers and dragons and stuff. Let's face it, there's probably a wizard in there somewhere, too. Maybe even multiple wizards. Gameplay, storyline and environment are all well considered, and there's even a multiplayer mode, enabling you to team up over Wi-Fi. Meanwhile, at the other end of the spectrum…

Gurk, the 8-bit RPG

It's like the last thirty years never happened. This old-school adventure has you exploring enchanted pixel forests and dungeons, battling blocky baddies as you go. It's surprisingly immersive. For more, there's **Gurk II**.

Sports & racing

Stair Dismount

Something for your inner psychopath? Look no further! Stair dismount has you scoring points by pushing a character down flights of stairs, off the ledges of huge structures and into bits of machinery. As he tumbles over the sharp corners and hard surfaces,

portions of your victim's limbs flash red to indicate a breakage, accompanied by delightful snapping and crumpling noises. You can also spice things up by grafting the face of your boss, ex or arch nemesis onto the hapless stair-crasher's head.

Flick Golf!

Here's your golfer, here's a golf club, here's a golf ball, there's the hole, now get to work! It's a simple premise for a game made even simpler by Flick Golf!'s intuitive controls: swipe the screen to swing and hit the ball. Once your ball is in flight, you can affect its trajectory by swiping a bit more demonstratively in the direction you'd like it to travel. Gameplay is very responsive and natural while presenting just the right amount of difficulty to keep you coming back for more.

Gnarbike Trials

Race through sixty increasingly difficult levels of ramps, tunnels and obstacles. The game's physics engine is realistic and controls consist of accelerate, brake, lean forward and lean back. If you tire (no pun intended) of the official levels you can construct your own, or play courses submitted by other users.

Glow Hockey 2

Vibrant, neon-lit air hockey table. Play against a friend, or a computer opponent at a variety of difficulty settings. Colourful, fast-paced and very playable. For more, try **Touch Hockey**.

Reckless Getaway

Can you outrun the cops? The fuzz? The filth? The rozzers? The pigs? Better put your foot down and smash your way through other traffic unfortunate enough to be sharing the road with you.

Pocket League Story

Soccer season simulation. Pick your team, train 'em up and play your way to the top of the league. You can't build a gym or stadium without some backing though, right? Right. Better shift some merch then, and start schmoozing up to those sponsors. Sadly, there's no option to gouge your fans with extortionate season ticket prices; maybe next time.

Stick Cricket

Cricket game. Pick your team, train 'em up… Some guy throws the ball at you, and you have to hit the ball with a bat. Controls are a simple case of swing left or swing right. It's about as interesting as the real thing. If you just can't get enough cricket, try **Cricket T20 Fever 3D**.

Virtual Table Tennis 3D

Table tennis game with surprisingly realistic and responsive paddling action. Difficulty is just right, so long as you're not trying to take a screen grab at the same time.

Arcade & action

Hungry Shark

Guide the gnarly dead-eyed predator through waters both shallow and deep, munching remorselessly on pelicans, shoals of fish and unsuspecting bathers. Head down to the ocean floor for tasty angler fish and other deep-sea treats, avoiding the mines and jellyfish. It's ugly, but fun.

Wind-up Knight

An immersive and well-paced 3D platform adventure game. Jump, slash and tumble your way through an increasingly challenging array of beautifully rendered obstacles. You'll need to collect every single coin in a level (no mean feat!) in order to buy your way onto the next. You also have the option of paying in actual real-life money if your impatience gets the better of you.

Annoying Orange: Carnage

Toss the terrified apples and bananas into the blender for pointless points. The orange, and by extension the whole game, is indeed annoying. For more fruit punishing, try **Fruit Ninja**.

Meganoid

Cute, pixelly platform game with simple left, right and jump buttons. Collect the diamonds, avoid the spikes and other obstacles, lather, rinse, repeat. This is one of a few apps by Orangepixel, all with a delightfully retro Gameboy-esque vibe.

SpaceCat (3D)

It's a cat in a flying saucer, as you'd expect. The objective is to navigate through ochre-tinted corridors while dodging obstacles and collecting squeaky mice. The game itself isn't really all that interesting, but when you accidentally knock your flying feline friend against a wall it holds its head in pain and makes a cute little anguished meow. Luckily (for you, not the cat), this happens constantly throughout the game and somehow manages to never get old.

Magnetic Shaving Derby

Drag razor-sharp, uh, razors, across this dismayed chap's bearded face with the help of a magnet, trying to avoid slicing through his nose, mouth or eyeballs. Get too rough and plumes of blood-red pixels gaily spew forth from his wounds, while a solitary tear rolls down his rugged, pixely cheek.

Naught

Atmospheric platform game with minimal silhouette-style artwork. Tilt your device to move the cat-like character around the screen, collecting diamonds. Things get interesting when you tilt too far; it turns out you can control the gravity within the game, moving the protagonist between floor and ceiling, or just free-falling it through the chambers and tunnels.

Doodle Jump

There's a seemingly endless line of jumping games being squeezed out by game developers, but this one could be regarded as something of an enduring classic. Leap the scrawly monster from platform to platform, collecting power-ups and dispensing baddies with nasal projectiles. For more upwardly mobile bouncing, try **GoGoGoat**. Or, for purists seeking an example of the genre distilled down to its most fundamental tropes, try **PapiJump**.

Hyper Jump

A more turbo-charged variation of the jumping game, this platformless escapade has you propelling a little critter upwards through a charmingly illustrated world. For more speed, less charm, try **Mega Jump**.

Chalk Ball

Kind of like Wipeout played on a blackboard. Keep the ball bouncing at the targets by

drawing lines underneath it, being careful not to run out of chalk. Different targets have different power-up effects, causing gravity to change directions, the ball to speed up, slow down and so on.

Robo Surf

Ride the waves with this adorable wee fella on a surf board. Collect oil barrels for a power boost while avoiding a flock of seagulls (no, not the band) and squaring up to various sub-aquatic end-of-level bosses. Simple to play, but utterly addictive.

Contract Killer

Everyone loves going on a killing spree, right? Well now you can act out that guilty pleasure in the virtual world without any of those nasty real-life consequences. Pick your weapon and choose a vantage point to start stealthily picking off the enemy one by one. For more satisfaction of your relentless bloodlust, try **Frontline Commando**, or if you feel more comfortable shooting at zombies, try **Contract Killer: Zombies (NR)**.

Fingerzilla

Still hungry for blood? Smash buildings down into smouldering heaps of rubble and squash their terrified occupants as they try to escape. Choose your weapon carefully; will you use your pinkie, middle finger or good old trusty index finger?

Classic

Andoku Sudoku 2

All the Sudoku you'll ever need, with ten thousand puzzles and six different kinds of game (standard, hyper, colour, percent, squiggly and X-sudoku, if that means anything to you). It also has eight difficulty levels, portrait and landscape modes, and can supply hints if you get stuck mid-game.

Random Mahjong

Luxurious recreation of this compelling ancient solitaire game. Remove pairs of available matching tiles as they become uncovered. Levels are generated randomly and range from relatively easy to incredibly challenging. We'd never played Mahjong before trying this out, and with the instructions included in the app it was easy to pick up.

Sounds, animations and backgrounds are all stunning, making this game an absolute pleasure to play.

Backgammon Free

Nicely designed and very playable backgammon board for two players, or one player against a fairly cunning computer opponent. Glowing hints allow you to focus on your available moves, which saves a lot of time staring blankly at the thing trying to figure it out.

Reversi Free

One of many Reversi games available, AI Factory's offering has ten difficulty levels and a two-player mode. For a slightly more pleasing interface and the ability to play online, try **Reversi** by Bluesky Studio.

Wordfeud

A popular alternative to Scrabble where you play online against millions of opponents worldwide (both Android™ and iPhone users). Along with built-in chat and the ability to play up to thirty games simultaneously (Really? Is that all?), Wordfeud adds a little extra spice by allowing you to randomize the position of letter and word score tiles. Also check out **Words With Friends**.

Solitaire MegaPack

Comprises 134 different solitaire games, well-known classics alongside more esoteric forms such as Osmosis, Beleaguered Castle, Algerian Patience and more.

RPS Combat

It's unclear how long the game of "Rock Paper Scissors" has been kicking around, but it almost certainly originated in ancient Egypt around 1500 BC, when the invention of scissors enabled the less successful "Rock Paper" (or "Rock Papyrus", as it was then known) to evolve into the sport we know and love. RPS Combat takes this evolution to the next level, allowing you to play a kind of Bad Luck Chess. Will it catch on? Check back in a couple more thousand years.

Index